Through the Psalms
with Derek Prince

Other Books by Derek Prince

Biography

Guides to the Life of Faith

Systematic Bible Exposition

Through the Psalms with Derek Prince

Derek Prince

Chosen Books

A Division of Baker Book House Co
Grand Rapids, Michigan 49516

© 1983 and 2002 by Derek Prince Ministries-International

Published by Chosen Books
a division of Baker Book House Company
P.O. Box 6287, Grand Rapids, MI 49516-6287

Printed in the United States of America

Previously published in 1983 under the title *Chords from David's Harp*.

Library of Congress Cataloging-in-Publication Data

Prince, Derek.
    Through the Psalms with Derek Prince / Derek Prince.
        p.   cm.
    Rev. ed. of : Chords from David's harp. 1983.
    Includes index.
    ISBN 0-8007-9305-6 (cloth)
    1. Bible. O.T. Psalms—Meditations. I. Prince, Derek.
Chords from David's harp. II. Title.
BS1430.4 .P74 2002
223' .206—dc21   2002002743

Cover photo
LYN89581
Sheep, 1991 (tempera on panel) by James Lynch (b.1956)
The Maas Gallery, London, UK/Bridgeman Art Library
COPYRIGHT MUST BE CLEARED

Introduction

David's harp has long been silent. Nor has history preserved any notational record of the music that he played. Probably none was ever set down in written form. It was preserved only in the memories of the musicians he trained, and by them passed down from generation to generation—until, with the destruction of the Second Temple, its music was finally silenced.

Nevertheless, the melodies of David's harp live on, not in the audible sounds of a musical instrument, but rather in the inner resonance of the soul that his psalms still call forth. In the succeeding centuries this response of the soul to David's psalms has become the experience of countless millions of people from all races and backgrounds and in every corner of the earth. How shall we describe this inner resonance? Perhaps the most appropriate word is *meditation*.

David's opening psalm pronounces a special blessing on the man who meditates on God's law day and night. David not only pronounces this blessing; he goes on to provide a limitless source of material to stimulate such meditation. There is no literature in the world that excels the psalms of David in the ability to provoke the human soul to meditate on the deepest and most abiding truths of God.

For more than sixty years I myself have turned again and again to the psalms of David. His writings have helped me, like millions of others, through the most trying times, including the loss of two wives—Lydia in 1975 and Ruth in 1999. At present I am battling on several fronts for my health, including a condition called polymyalgia that has greatly reduced my physical strength. Yet the Psalms still supply the needs of my soul— encouragement, inspiration, correction, inner strength and vision. It is my sincere prayer that these brief personal meditations will in turn stimulate my readers to meditations of their own that will go far beyond anything that I have here been able to set down in writing. Meditation on the law of God is a limitless ocean of delight, of which only the shallowest borders may ever be communicated from one soul to another. The fullness of the ocean can find expression only in the soul's most intimate communion with God Himself.

The meditations in this book are set forth in the order of the passages from the psalms on which they are based, beginning at Psalm 1 and continuing on to the last passage, which is taken from Psalm 147. Many readers will probably wish to follow this order, perhaps commencing, or closing, each day with a meditation.

It may also be, however, that at times a reader will be searching for a meditation to suit some special mood or situation. To meet this need I have provided—on pages 213 to 220—an index of all the material in the book under seven headings:

1. God's Eternal Majesty
2. Prayer and Praise
3. Learning God's Ways
4. Times of Pressure
5. God's All-Embracing Care
6. The Word at Work
7. Time and Eternity

Quite a number of the meditations are listed under more than one heading. Many of those listed under "Times of Pressure," for example, are also included in "Learning God's Ways." This in itself illustrates an important practical lesson: It is often in *times of pressure* that we most quickly and effectively *learn God's ways.* It also serves to bring out the many-faceted nature of the Psalms. Even a short verse of one or two lines may provide insight into several precious aspects of divine truth.

> The law of the LORD is perfect,
>   reviving the soul.
> The statutes of the LORD are trustworthy,
>   making wise the simple.
> The precepts of the LORD are right,
>   giving joy to the heart.
> The commands of the LORD are radiant,
>   giving light to the eyes.
>
>   Psalm 19:7–8

May the meditations that follow help you to receive your full portion! May they revive your soul, make you wise, give joy to your heart and light to your eyes!

Derek Prince
Jerusalem
January 2002

Through the Psalms

Blessed Prosperity

Blessed is the man
    who does not walk in the counsel of the
    wicked
or stand in the way of sinners
    or sit in the seat of mockers.
But his delight is in the law of the Lord,
    and on his law he meditates day and night.
He is like a tree planted by streams of water,
    which yields its fruit in season
and whose leaf does not wither.
    Whatever he does prospers.

Psalm 1:1–3

"Blessed"; the opening word of the Psalms contains the essence of all that is to follow. The blessings they unfold flow in two directions: from God to man, and from man back again to God.

David goes on to sum up the blessedness promised to man in one brief, expressive sentence: "Whatever he does prospers." How can you be such a person—blessed of God so that whatever you do prospers? David lays down five conditions, the first three negative, the last two positive.

First, the negative: you must *not* walk in the counsel of the wicked; you must *not* stand in the way of sinners; you must *not* sit in the seat of mockers. There is one decisive issue: from where do you get your counsel? The counsel you follow determines the course of your life. If your counsel comes from the people who reject God's principles and flout His requirements, you can have no claim upon His blessing.

Next, the positive: you must delight in the law of the Lord and you must meditate on it day and night. The ultimate source of all wise and righteous counsel is the law of the Lord. If you fill your heart and mind continually with His law, and if you direct your life according to it, then blessing and prosperity are your God-appointed portion.

Perhaps you are weary of frustration and failure. Then take heed to these rules. Meditate on them. Apply them. They will work in your life. God Himself guarantees you success.

Faith's Response

Lord, I will follow the example of David and say, "Your statutes are my delight; they are my counselors" (Psalm 119:24).

with Derek Prince

The Gift of Sleep

I lie down and sleep;
   I wake again, because the L<small>ORD</small> sustains me.
I will not fear the tens of thousands
   drawn up against me on every side.

Psalm 3:5–6

I will lie down and sleep in peace,
   for you alone, O L<small>ORD</small>,
   make me dwell in safety.

Psalm 4:8

He grants sleep to those he loves.

Psalm 127:2

One of the beautiful revelations of Scripture is that sleep is a gift of God for those He loves. David found himself under tremendous pressures, surrounded by enemies on every side, his very life threatened. He speaks of "tens of thousands drawn up against me on every side." Yet in the midst of it all he knows the blessedness of untroubled, restful sleep.

He gives two reasons: "Because the LORD sustains me" and again, "For you alone, O LORD, make me dwell in safety." His security depended solely on the Lord—not on circumstances, or on material provisions, or on the fragile promises of men, but on the eternal, unchanging promises of God's Word.

Each night he committed himself to the Lord. He lay down in confidence in the Lord. He knew that his soul was safe in the Lord's keeping. He could sleep and he could awake without anxiety, without fear, without the torment of sleeplessness.

There are many today who do not have this blessed assurance. When nighttime comes, they are distressed, perplexed, fearful. The worries and cares of the day follow them into the night. If you are one of these, take a lesson from David. Recognize in God Himself your all-sufficient source of security and peace. Then accept by simple faith His love gift of sleep.

Faith's Response

Lord, I believe that You love me and that You have for me, too, your blessed gift of sleep.

The Source of Joy

Many are asking, "Who can show us any
  good?"
  Let the light of your face shine upon us, O
  LORD,
You have filled my heart with greater joy
  than when their grain and new wine abound.

Psalm 4:6–7

How true that is of our situation today! Many
indeed are asking, "Who can show us any good?"
There is a kind of disillusionment in the air—a per-
vasive sense of pessimism. This is particularly true
in the realm of politics. There is a dearth of confidence in leadership, the aftermath of an agoniz-
ing series of mismanaged crises that have passed
over us in recent decades.

Yet there is an answer to the question "Who can
show us any good?"—an answer that is still valid
today. David himself provides the answer, for he
continues, "Let the light of your face shine upon
us, O LORD." Real goodness has only one source.
It comes from the Lord. When He lifts up the light

of His face upon us, that light dispels the darkness of uncertainty and insecurity and pessimism.

Instead, we are filled with joy—"greater joy than when their grain and new wine abound." For those whose outlook is limited to the material realm, contentment and security must be measured in terms of material abundance. But for those who have learned to look in faith to God, there is another Source, inexhaustible and unfluctuating. The satisfaction it offers excels anything we can obtain from mere material abundance.

"Every good and perfect gift is from above, coming down from the Father of the heavenly lights, who does not change like shifting shadows" (James 1:17).

Faith's Response

Let the light of Your face shine upon me, Lord, so that I may see and enjoy the abundance of Your provision.

Beginning Your Day

In the morning, O Lᴏʀᴅ, you hear my voice;
in the morning I lay my requests before you
and wait in expectation.

Psalm 5:3

How does your day begin? Do you start with a
scramble, with a flurry, trying to do three different things at one time? Do you find yourself often
short of breath and short of temper, impatient with
your wife or your husband, scolding the kids, anx-
ious, unable to cope? Do you go out into the day
unprepared, ill-armed, not altogether confident of
what lies ahead of you?

The reason is simple: You do not begin your day
aright. Take a lesson from David: "In the morning,
O Lᴏʀᴅ, you hear my voice." The first thing David
did each morning was to lift his voice to the Lord.
His first words of the day were addressed to God,
not to man.

He goes on, "In the morning I lay my requests
before you and wait in expectation." What a wise
way to begin the day! Lift your voice to God in

prayer. Lay your requests before Him. Set out before Him the things you are going to have to do that day. Commit to Him the problems, the difficulties you anticipate. Submit your decisions to Him. Then, like David, you will be able to wait in expectation. You will go out to meet the day fully armed, confidently expecting the answers to those prayers that you laid before God in the morning.

There is a Greek proverb that says, "The beginning is half of the whole." Certainly that is true of making our way through each day. The way we begin determines nearly all that is to follow. Seldom will the day's end be more blessed than its beginning. So begin each day by letting God hear your voice.

Faith's Response

Help me, Lord, to begin each day aright, by letting You hear my voice and by laying my requests before You.

True Security

For surely, O LORD, you bless the righteous;
   you surround them with your favor as with
   a shield.

Psalm 5:12

David was sure of one thing: God blesses the righteous. We need to be no less sure. Today many sources to which we looked for security and certainty have failed us. Trusted political and financial institutions are crumbling around us. But there is one thing in life that is still sure: God blesses the righteous.

This simple, unchanging fact has important practical implications for the way we live. On the one hand, we need to devote less time and effort to making provision for material security. On the other hand, we need to be more concerned about making sure our lives are right before God; that we qualify for that blessing of the Lord which He reserves for the righteous—and only for the righteous.

The blessing of the Lord also brings His protection with it. David says, "You surround them [the

righteous] with your favor as with a shield." God's favor is toward the righteous. When we cultivate His righteousness, then His favor encircles us like a shield on all sides. It shields us against the blows and the pressures of life. It comes between us and the forces of evil that seek to destroy us—forces too powerful and cunning for us to deal with in our own strength or wisdom. We have no protection against these forces except the invisible but also invincible shield that is the Lord's favor.

In the light of these unchanging laws that govern our lives, we need to reexamine our priorities. Righteousness pays better—and more enduring—dividends than cleverness or expediency or self-interest.

"But seek first his kingdom and his righteousness, and all these things will be given to you as well" (Matthew 6:33).

Faith's Response

Help me, Lord, to be more concerned about righteousness than about success or expediency.

Prevailing Through Praise

> From the lips of children and infants
> you have ordained praise
> because of your enemies,
> to silence the foe and the avenger.

Psalm 8:2

Throughout the Book of Psalms David refers continually to his enemies. Few men had more enemies than David. Persistently they pursued him and surrounded him, seeking his destruction. He survived only because he learned the secret of dealing with his enemies. He did not meet them in his own power or wisdom. Rather, he invoked against them the presence and power of God.

One main way that he did this was through praise. This was the way God Himself ordained, for David says, "From the lips of children and infants you have ordained praise . . . to silence the foe and the avenger." In the natural order, children and infants are the weakest of all. But when praise comes from even the weakest, its effect is to silence the foe and the avenger.

The Bible reveals that we, too, like David, are surrounded by enemies, though ours are primarily in the unseen spiritual realm. The chief of these enemies is "the foe and the avenger"—Satan himself. He is the accuser of the brothers, the one who misrepresents us, who misinterprets everything we do, who even seeks to accuse us before the very throne of God.

How can we silence him? David has shown us the way: by praise. When our praise ascends to God, it silences Satan. It cancels his accusations and stops his mouth. It leaves us free to live out our lives without the continual condemnation of his accusations. Through praise we invoke the presence and power of our God against all the forces that oppose us.

Faith's Response

Along with my prayers, Lord, I offer You my praise, believing that together they will prevail over all the opposition of Satan.

On Center Stage

When I consider your heavens,
   the work of your fingers,
the moon and the stars,
   which you have set in place,
what is man that you are mindful of him,
   the son of man that you care for him?

Psalm 8:3–4

When we look up at the vastness of the heavens and consider their millions of galaxies, our earthly globe seems just a tiny speck of dust in the totality of the universe. Confronted by this vastness, we feel small and insignificant, weak and helpless.

And yet, David assures us, God is interested in us. He cares for us. In fact, we are the objects of His special attention. God does not measure everything by numbers or dimensions. He has another scale of values, according to which—as Jesus Himself told us—one human soul is worth more than the entire universe.

We have often tended to picture our earth as the center of the universe. In all probability this is not so. Yet, historically, it has been something

more important—the stage on which the greatest dramas of the universe have been acted out, and are still being acted out.

It was on the stage of earth and in the city of Jerusalem two thousand years ago that the drama of redemption was enacted. God demonstrated to the universe the value that He set upon human souls. He offered for our redemption the most precious thing the universe contained—the lifeblood of His own Son. Appropriately, therefore, Paul writes, "We have been made a spectacle to the whole universe . . ." (1 Corinthians 4:9). The word here translated *spectacle* is actually the Greek word for "theatre."

Weak and unworthy though we may be in ourselves, yet in the sovereign purposes of God we occupy the very center of the stage of the universe.

Faith's Response

Thank You, Lord, that You are more concerned about us, Your children, than about the entire universe that surrounds us.

"To the Shelter"

> In the LORD I take refuge.
>> How then can you say to me:
>> "Flee like a bird to your mountain" . . . ?
>
> Psalm 11:1

What is your place of refuge? Are you disturbed when people challenge you? Or when you look around at the turmoil and instability of the world in which we live? Jesus warned us that, as this age draws to its close, we will "hear of wars and revolutions," and that "men will faint from terror, apprehensive of what is coming on the world" (Luke 21:9, 26).

All this teaches us that we need a place of refuge. In all the dwelling places of modern Israel, from the largest cities to the smallest villages and settlements, there is one universal sign painted in red or black on the walls of the buildings: *To the Shelter*. A generation of war and threats of war has imprinted on the minds of the people of Israel one vital lesson: *Every person needs a place of refuge*.

David said, "In the LORD I take refuge." He had a place of refuge, and he knew it. He was not intimidated by the dangers that confronted him. Rather, he challenged those who questioned whether such a refuge was sufficient. He asked them, "How can you tell me to flee like a bird to my mountain?"

For these people the "mountain" was the visible emblem of strength and stability. It seemed ridiculous and impractical to them to seek refuge in something invisible and spiritual—something they could not apprehend with their physical senses. Many people today have the same outlook. For their security they look only to the material world and to human resources.

Yet God Himself warns us, "The mountains shall depart, and the hills be removed; but my kindness shall not depart from thee . . ." (Isaiah 54:10 KJV).

Where is your place of refuge?

Faith's Response

I will say of the Lord, "He is my refuge and my fortress, my God, in whom I trust" (Psalm 91:2).

Refined in a Furnace

And the words of the LORD are flawless,
like silver refined in a furnace of clay,
purified seven times.

Psalm 12:6

These are the words that are brought to us in Scripture. They are flawless—without error, totally and absolutely reliable. Do you perhaps wonder at that statement, knowing that these words have come to us through human agents, men who were weak and fallible, and who made many mistakes? (Often, in fact, their mistakes were actually recorded in Scripture.) How then can it be that the Bible's message is absolutely infallible and authoritative?

To answer this question, David presents us with a vivid picture—a picture of silver being purified in an oven of clay. (Such clay ovens are still used among the people of the Middle East today.) In David's picture there are three main elements: the furnace of clay; the silver that is to be purified; and the purifying fire.

The furnace of clay represents the human instruments through whom the message of Scripture is brought. The silver represents the message itself. The purifying fire represents the work of the Holy Spirit. The silver is purified "seven times." In Scripture the number seven is particularly associated with the Holy Spirit. In his vision on Patmos, for example, John saw the Holy Spirit as "seven lamps of fire" (Revelation 4:5 KJV). Secondarily, the number seven suggests completeness or perfection.

As the words of Scripture come to us through the furnace of human clay, they have been completely purified by the fire of the Holy Spirit. The "dross" of human error has been fully purged. Thus they are flawless.

"For prophecy never had its origin in the will of man, but men spoke from God as they were carried along by the Holy Spirit" (2 Peter 1:21).

Faith's Response

The law from your mouth is more precious to me than thousands of pieces of silver and gold (Psalm 119:72).

The Wonderful Counselor

I will praise the LORD, who counsels me;
even at night my heart instructs me.

Psalm 16:7

I can echo those words of David. I know what it is
to have access to the Lord's counsel, and I value it
above all human wisdom. I have proven many
times in my own experience that the Lord's counsel is reliable. Later on in the revelation of Scripture, Isaiah describes the Lord as a Wonderful
Counselor (Isaiah 9:6). The word translated *Wonderful* always contains in it an element of the supernatural. The Lord's counsel is on a level higher than
that of human wisdom, human insight, human
knowledge. I am so grateful to have access to His
counsel!

I can echo, too, those words that follow in the
next line: "Even at night my heart instructs me."
Many times when I have an unresolved problem,
I simply commit it to the Lord and go to sleep,
without wrestling any further with it. Then in the
stillness of the night the Lord awakens me. In the

innermost depths of my heart, with that still, small voice, He speaks to me and shows me the answer to my problem.

How good it is to know that you have access to the counsel of the Lord! When you have come to the end of your own ability, when you have reasoned everything out and it still makes no sense, when you find yourself at an impasse in your life and you do not know which way to turn, remember that the Lord is the Wonderful Counselor! Go to Him. Commit your problem to Him. Open your heart to Him—for He speaks to the heart, not to the head. In His own wonderful way, He will show you the answer.

Faith's Response

You guide me with your counsel, and afterward you will take me into glory (Psalm 73:24).

Clothed in Righteousness

As for me, I shall behold Your face in
   righteousness;
I will be satisfied with Your likeness when I
   awake.

Psalm 17:15 NASB

What beautiful words! What a beautiful expectation! It is the expectation of every true believer—one that extends beyond the end of time and out into eternity. We will fall asleep in death, but one day we will awake. And when we awake, we will be satisfied—satisfied with the likeness of the Lord. We will find ourselves clothed with His righteousness. We will put on His likeness. We will behold His face.

That one word *satisfied* sounds a chord in the depths of my being. I like to repeat it to myself. "I will be satisfied—satisfied—fully satisfied!" For this I am prepared both to work and to wait—if need be, to suffer also.

I do not believe there is anything else that can fully satisfy the human heart, except God Himself.

At this time, in this life, as believers, we have contact with God, we know Him, we serve Him, we do His will. But there are gaps in the revelation. There is a veil in between. We are still creatures of flesh. Our ideas and our concepts are so limited, and so inadequate to apprehend God.

But there is coming a day when we will awake clothed in His righteousness, not in our own, to stand faultless before His throne and to see Him face-to-face. And then we will be satisfied! Nothing else can take the place of that. That is the end of all living. It all ends in God Himself.

"To him who is able to keep you from falling and to present you before his glorious presence without fault and with great joy—to the only God our Savior be glory, majesty, power and authority, through Jesus Christ our Lord, before all ages, now and forevermore! Amen" (Jude 24–25).

Faith's Response

Lord, I renounce any earthly satisfaction that would rob me of the satisfaction of beholding Your face in righteousness.

Open Before God

> To the faithful you show yourself faithful,
>   to the blameless you show yourself
>   blameless,
> to the pure you show yourself pure,
>   but to the crooked you show yourself
>   shrewd.

Psalm 18:25–26

David here unfolds a deep and abiding principle of God's dealings with us: The way we relate to God determines the way God in turn relates to us. David pictures four attributes of character: faithful, blameless, pure and crooked. Whichever of these attributes we manifest in our dealings with God calls forth a corresponding aspect of God's nature toward us.

Do we desire to prove God's faithfulness? The way to do this is to cultivate faithfulness toward God. If we are faithful to Him, He will be more than faithful to us. Scripture and experience alike affirm: God is faithful. He rewards every act of sincere faith, no matter how small or humble.

On this basis of faith—or faithfulness, we need to develop two further attributes of character that David mentions: blamelessness and purity. Alternative translations for *blameless* are "perfect" or "complete" or "wholehearted." To be wholehearted and pure in our relationship with God means that we conceal nothing from Him, withhold nothing from Him, and renounce all that displeases or offends Him. The measure in which we open ourselves to God determines the measure of God's fullness that He, in turn, makes available to us. If there are no reservations on our side, there will be none on God's side either.

But then there is that final word of warning: "To the crooked you show yourself shrewd." I have met people who have convinced themselves that they can somehow make God a partner to their own crooked schemes. It never works that way! God proves Himself much shrewder than they.

"Do not be deceived: God cannot be mocked. A man reaps what he sows" (Galatians 6:7).

Faith's Response

I will open my heart and life to God in the same measure that I desire to receive from Him.

God Is Alive!

The LORD lives! Praise be to my Rock!
Exalted be God my Savior!

Psalm 18:46

Sometimes the shortest sentences state the most important facts. "The LORD lives!" God is alive! This one simple statement is more significant than all the complicated formulae in all the books of theology that have ever been written.

At one time Martin Luther was facing such overwhelming opposition, both human and satanic, that he began to lose his confidence in God and in himself and to give way to despair. One day his wife, Käthe, appeared at the breakfast table completely attired in the traditional black garb of mourning. "Why are you wearing mourning today?" Luther asked her.

"Because God is dead," she replied.

"Nonsense, woman," Luther said, "God is not dead."

"Well, if God is not dead," Käthe rejoined, "why do you act as if He is?"

Käthe's rebuke helped Luther to regain a proper spiritual focus, and with it his confidence in God and in himself. He realized that as long as God lives, no situation is hopeless and no problem insoluble.

More recently someone has expressed the same thought in mathematical terms: One plus God is always a majority.

Some time back there was a school of theology identified by the slogan: *God is dead*. History has proved them wrong. Today that school of theology is dead. Many of the theologians who espoused it are probably dead, too. But God lives on.

Because God lives, He is both a Rock and a Savior. As a Rock, He is unchanging and impregnable. As a Savior, He offers forgiveness and eternal security.

Faith's Response

As long as God lives, I will live, for God is my life.

A Throne for the King

Yet You are holy,
O You who are enthroned upon the praises of
Israel.

Psalm 22:3 NASB

Here is an insight that can revolutionize our attitude toward prayer and worship: *The throne upon which God sits is the praises of His people.* In heaven God already has a throne that is established forever. But when He leaves His heavenly throne to come among His people on earth, then our praises become His throne. God is King forever, whether we praise Him or not. We do not make Him a king by praising Him. But we offer Him the throne that is His due.

Jesus promised His disciples, "Where two or three come together in my name, there am I with them" (Matthew 18:20). His presence in our midst is guaranteed. It depends upon His faithfulness, not our response. But when He comes into our midst as King of kings and Lord of lords, it is right and appropriate that we respond to Him as King. As King, He merits a throne. Nothing else becomes Him. It is our privilege to offer Him the throne. When we praise Him and exalt Him, when we glorify His name and extol His majesty, we are acknowledging His kingship. We are responding appropriately. We are offering Him the throne that is His due.

Not only is this response of praise appropriate to the One whom we worship. It will also change our attitude and enlarge our faith. The more we praise Him, the more clearly we apprehend His kingly wisdom and power. Then it takes no effort to exercise faith for the answers to our prayers. It becomes natural to believe that this glorious King is both willing and able to do what we ask of Him.

Faith's Response

Help me, Lord, that I may never fail to offer You the throne of praise that is Your due.

One All-Sufficient Relationship

The LORD is my shepherd, I shall not lack.

Psalm 23:1 AMP

I never read those familiar words without marveling. Familiarity has never diminished their impact. What tremendous confidence David had! What absolute security! "I shall not lack." There will never arise a need in my life for which I shall not have the supply, no matter what the need may be. Whether it be spiritual, physical or financial, the supply is guaranteed. "I shall not lack!"

If David had added anything to his statement, he would have spoiled it. If he had said, "I shall not lack money, or food, or health, or clothes"— or whatever else—he would have set limits to his statement. But he left it unlimited. "I shall not lack"—period!

What was the secret of David's assurance? Is it possible for you and me to share that assurance? David's secret is very simple, very clear: "The LORD

is my shepherd." That was the sole and sufficient basis of David's assurance.

It is not a statement of doctrine, but of a relationship—an intimate personal relationship with the Lord.

The statement is in the present tense—"The Lord *is* my shepherd"—not "was," not "will be." David is not looking back to the past, or ahead to the future. He focuses on the immediate present. Here and now—just at this moment—the Lord *is* my shepherd. Just two persons are involved—the Lord and David.

On the basis of a similar relationship, each of us may have a similar assurance. Here and now I am related to the Lord as my shepherd. Out of that relationship I have total security. I know that all my needs will be supplied.

Faith's Response

Lord, I affirm that You are indeed my shepherd, and I thank You for the assurance that all my needs will be supplied.

The Valley
of the Shadow

> Even though I walk
>   through the valley of the shadow of death,
> I will fear no evil,
>   for you are with me;
> your rod and your staff,
>   they comfort me.

Psalm 23:4

Everything David says in this psalm is the out-working of the opening statement: "The Lord is my shepherd." It all flows out of his direct, personal relationship to the Lord as his shepherd.

Here David speaks of what this relationship means to him when he walks through "the valley of the shadow of death." God does not guarantee us that we will never walk through this valley. In fact, David's words imply that at some time or other we will. Nor do I believe that "the valley of the shadow of death" is only, or primarily, the experience of physical death when our life on earth ends. Elsewhere in Scripture the same phrase,

the shadow of death, is applied to situations in this present life.

I believe there can be many occasions in this life when we walk through this valley of the shadow: occasions of bereavement, loneliness, sickness, persecution, discouragement. The Lord does not promise that we will not walk through this kind of valley. But He does promise to be with us. In particular, He makes His rod and His staff continually available to us. The rod represents discipline; the staff represents support. It is significant that the rod comes before the staff. If we want God's support, we must first submit to His discipline. On that basis, His presence with us is guaranteed even in the darkest valley.

Faith's Response

Lord, I gladly receive both Your rod and Your staff. When I come to the valley, I know I will not be alone.

God's Banquet Table

You prepare a table before me
   in the presence of my enemies.
You anoint my head with oil;
   my cup overflows.

Psalm 23:5

All that is contained in this verse flows, just as the previous verses do, from the great basic relationship stated in the opening verse: "The Lᴏʀᴅ is my shepherd." Once this relationship has been established in our lives, the outworking of it can be the same for each of us as it was for David.

The fifth verse—here quoted—unfolds three main aspects of God's provision for us: a prepared table; our head anointed with oil; our cup overflowing. At first we might conclude that all this indicates a situation in which everything is going just the way we want and we have no problems and no opposition. But the very opposite is the case! All this bounteous provision of God is made available to us "in the presence of our enemies." It is important to realize that the presence of our

enemies cannot keep us from enjoying God's complete provision for us.

On the contrary, it is in just such a situation that God especially delights to demonstrate both His power and His abundance. In the presence of our enemies God spreads His banquet for us. Then He says to our enemies: "This is my provision for My children. They will enjoy it right before your eyes, and you will not be able to harm them or take it from them."

Sometimes, however, we are tempted to take our eyes off the Lord and focus on our enemies. Then we begin to say, "If it were not for my enemies, I know that God would bless me and provide for me." Instead our attitude should be, "Because of my enemies I am expecting God's best."

Faith's Response

I will not let fear of my enemies keep me from enjoying God's best, wherever He provides it for me.

From Enrollment
to Graduation

> What man is he that feareth the LORD?
> him shall he teach in the way that he shall
> choose. . . .
> The secret of the LORD is with them that fear
> him . . .

Psalm 25:12, 14 KJV

When God sets out to teach man, He chooses His students on the basis of character—not intellectual ability, or academic degrees, or social standing. He looks for an inner attitude of the heart toward Himself: reverent submission and respect.

Furthermore, God sets the curriculum. He teaches such a man "in the way that he [God] shall choose." Often this is not the way we would choose for ourselves. We might incline toward themes of prophecy or revelation that seem profound, whereas God's curriculum might focus on what is humble and down-to-earth: service, sacrifice, faithfulness.

For those who submit to God's instruction, there is a wonderful reward: "The secret of the LORD is

with them that fear him." In human relationships, we share our secrets only with those we trust. Likewise, when God shares His secrets with us, it is proof we have earned His trust. It is our certificate of graduation.

This is beautifully illustrated in the relationship of Jesus to His disciples. After He had put them through three years of rigorous discipline, He told them: "I no longer call you servants, because a servant does not know his master's business. Instead, I have called you friends, for everything that I learned from my Father I have made known to you" (John 15:15). First, Jesus Himself learned from the Father through perfect submission to Him. Then He in turn passed on all He had learned from the Father to those who submitted in like manner to Him.

God still chooses His students on the same basis. Neither His requirements nor His curriculum have changed.

Faith's Response

Lord, I desire to be such a student that in Your time You will share Your secrets with me.

You Can Be His Temple!

And in His temple everything says, "Glory!"

Psalm 29:9 NASB

Within your temple, O God,
we meditate on your unfailing love.

Psalm 48:9

What sets God's temple apart from every other place in the universe? It is a place where there is only one theme: God and His glory. Everything in the temple says, "Glory!" Not just the living worshipers—the angelic beings, the cherubim and the seraphim—but even the furniture and the structure itself joins in the cry: "Glory to God!" Together they make up a single unit of worship.

However, the worship in God's temple is not limited to outward verbal expression. It is carried on simultaneously in the inner, unvoiced meditation of the soul. The theme of this inner meditation is God's unfailing love. The beautiful Hebrew word thus translated has been rendered in many ways: mercy, lovingkindness, goodness. . . . Each of these

Through the Psalms

conveys part of the meaning, but even taken together they do not fully express the whole. It constitutes an inexhaustible theme for the meditation of the true worshiper.

These are the two distinctive marks of God's temple: verbal worship proclaiming His glory, and inner meditation focused on His unfailing love. Whenever we meet these conditions, whenever our whole being cries, "Glory to God!" and all our thoughts are focused on His unfailing love, then we become God's temple. It may be in an automobile, or an office, or a kitchen. The physical location is not important.

Right where you are just now, you can become a temple of God! Focus your heart and mind on His unfailing love. Then open your lips and praise Him. Let your whole being unite in a single cry: "Glory!"

Faith's Response

Lord, in the depths of my being I meditate on Your unfailing love; my mouth proclaims Your glory.

Enthroned
over the Flood

The LORD sits enthroned over the flood;
  the LORD is enthroned as King forever.
The LORD gives strength to his people;
  the LORD blesses his people with peace.

Psalm 29:10–11

David here presents the Lord as a mighty King on His throne. We see Him enthroned over the restless, raging waters of a flood. These speak to us of tremendous forces unleashed all around us, which threaten our very lives, but which we cannot control. These raging waters also typify the restless, rebellious nations of the world under the dominion of evil spiritual powers. In his vision on Patmos John saw a prostitute sitting on many waters, and he was told, "The waters you saw, where the prostitute sits, are peoples, multitudes, nations and languages" (Revelation 17:15). These, too, are hostile to us, as God's people.

Against this background of raging, hostile forces, David reminds us that there is a King who rules

over them all. It is the Lord. He waits for us to recognize His kingship and to give Him the praise and glory that are His due. When we do this, He in turn responds to us in two ways: He gives us His strength and He blesses us with His peace.

The strength that will uphold us in the midst of all these hostile forces comes only from the Lord. Our own will fail us, but "those who hope in the LORD will renew their strength" (Isaiah 40:31). In the midst of the pressures, too, the Lord blesses His people with peace. Peace does not depend upon external circumstances. It comes from acknowledging the Lord enthroned over the flood.

Faith's Response

Lord, I lift my eyes from the flood to You on Your throne above, and I draw from You the strength and peace that I need.

Call for Help!

O LORD my God, I called to you for help
and you healed me.

Psalm 30:2

One of the things that blesses me about the Bible
is its profound simplicity. It comes out with the
most profound statements in the simplest and
shortest words. In the verse here quoted there is
not a single word of more than one syllable. Four-
teen words of one syllable, yet in those simple
words what tremendous truth is expressed!

All through the Bible God reveals Himself as the
healer of His people. To Israel, after their deliverance from Egypt, He declared, "I am the LORD, who
heals you" (Exodus 15:26). This could be translated: "I am the LORD your Doctor." Twelve centuries later He affirmed, "I the LORD do not change"
(Malachi 3:6).

To Christians in the New Testament James
wrote: "Is any one of you sick? He should call the
elders of the church to pray over him and anoint
him with oil in the name of the Lord. And the

prayer offered in faith will make the sick person well; the Lord will raise him up" (James 5:14–15).

I thank God for doctors and nurses and all who help the sick and the infirm. But the ultimate healer is God Himself. The channels of healing may vary, but the Source is always the same.

Perhaps you are laboring under some sickness, some physical oppression, some burden from which the Lord would gladly release you. Have you thought about calling to the Lord? Consider the simplicity of those words: "I called to you for help and you healed me." Sometimes we overlook that which is so simple and so close at hand.

Why not take your case to God? I have done it many times and He has healed me. I believe He will do the same for you.

Faith's Response

Lord, You are my Creator and my Redeemer. As I trust You to save my soul, so also I trust You to heal my body.

The Lord of Time

But I trust in you, O Lᴏʀᴅ;
    I say, "You are my God."
My times are in your hands. . . .

Psalm 31:14–15

What a profound and blessed revelation, that God has absolute control over all the times in our lives! Alone in the universe, God controls time totally. This is beautifully demonstrated in the heavenly bodies. Countless millions of stars rotate endlessly with absolute precision. They never collide. None of them ever departs from its appointed path or its appointed schedule.

All this is not the expression of some mindless mechanical process. On the contrary, it reveals God's personal involvement in the universe that He has created. He Himself names each star and watches over its course. Isaiah reminds us that it is "he who brings out the starry host one by one, and calls them each by name. Because of his great power and mighty strength, not one of them is missing" (Isaiah 40:26).

Through the Psalms

Just as accurately and as perfectly as God controls the movements of the stars, He also controls the courses of our lives. In particular, He controls the time element in each of our lives. He foresees each situation before it arises. Some sudden crisis may perhaps find us unprepared—but never God. In and through it all, He consistently and unhurriedly works out His own purpose for us.

For me personally, time has always been the element in life that I have found hardest to control—much harder, for instance, than money. The solution, I have learned, is to yield full control of time to God—to say with David, "My times are in your hands." At the beginning of each day I pray specifically that throughout that day I may "always be in the right place at the right time." From then on the events of my day follow God's schedule as surely as the stars in their courses.

Faith's Response

Lord, I ask You—and I trust You—to control the times in my life just as surely as You control the stars in heaven.

Blessed Forgiveness

Blessed is he
  whose transgressions are forgiven,
  whose sins are covered.
Blessed is the man
  whose sin the LORD does not count
  against him
  and in whose spirit is no deceit.

Psalm 32:1–2

In the original Hebrew, the opening word of each of these verses, "blessed," is in the plural. We might render it: "Oh, the blessednesses of the man . . . !" Yet all these multiplied "blessednesses" are available to every one of us. No one is excluded. Do you realize why? Because there is not one of us who has not sinned. Here is a divine paradox: It is the very fact that we have sinned that opens up for us all these "blessednesses."

There are three things that David says God will do for us. First, He will forgive our transgressions; He will release us from all guilt. Second, He will cover our sins; He will expunge from the record every sin we have ever committed. Third, He will

not count our sin against us; every debt we have incurred by our sin will be canceled. We will be free to make a totally new start, just as though we had never committed a single sin.

In return, God imposes only one condition—a condition indicated by the final phrase: "in whose spirit is no deceit." God does require sincerity, honesty, openness. We dare not put on a religious act; we dare not try to cover up or excuse. Simply and sincerely we acknowledge that we have sinned and deserve God's judgment. But we turn from our sin, we confess it—and God forgives!

Oh, let us cultivate the habit of being honest with God!

Faith's Response

Lord, I open up to You my whole heart and life. I cover nothing; I offer no excuse. I simply trust You to forgive.

The Creative Word

By the word of the LORD were the heavens made,
  their starry host by the breath of his mouth. . . .
For he spoke, and it came to be;
  he commanded, and it stood firm.

Psalm 33:6, 9

Ever since human history began, men have spec-
ulated as to the origin of the universe. What was
the "first cause"? How did it all come into being?
Endless theories have been (and are still being)
offered. But the psalmist here reveals the real
"first cause" of the universe: the word of the Lord
and the breath (literally, *spirit*) of His mouth. Everything that was ever created came into being
when the Lord spoke the word, and the breath—
or spirit—of His mouth was united with that
word.

This is illustrated vividly in the opening verses
of Genesis. Verse 2: "The Spirit of God was mov-
ing over the surface of the waters. . . ." Verse 3:
"Then God said, 'Let there be light'; and there was
light" (NASB).

At that moment God's word was united with His spirit. Their union brought into being that which God spoke. He uttered the word *light,* and light itself came into being. "He spoke, and it came to be; he commanded, and it stood firm." The Lord spoke the universe into being. Through the union of His word and His spirit creation was accomplished. Nothing more was needed.

What limitless possibilities are contained in this revelation! Each time we open our hearts to God's Word and Spirit, working together, the same power is released within us that brought the entire universe into being. God's Word will reproduce itself in our experience just as surely as it brought forth light on creation's first day.

Faith's Response

Thank You, Lord, for Your creative power at work within me as I yield to Your Spirit and obey Your Word.

Delivered from Fear

I sought the Lord, and he answered me;
   he delivered me from all my fears.
Those who look to him are radiant;
   their faces are never covered with shame.

Psalm 34:4–5

That is the testimony of personal experience. It is not theory. It is not theology. It is not even a creed. It is the testimony of a man in a difficult and dangerous situation. He turned to the Lord; he sought the Lord in prayer; and his testimony is: "The Lord answered me and delivered me from all my fears."

Are you oppressed with fear? Are you like the majority of people in our contemporary culture who have some kind of fear that gnaws at them, that takes away their peace? Why not try David's remedy? Seek the Lord! Pray to Him and ask Him to deliver you from all your fears.

Up to this point David has been speaking out of his own personal experience. He now goes on to make a more general statement—based, I suppose,

on his observation of people he has known: "Those who look to him [the Lord] are radiant. . . ."

David here touches on an important practical principle: Our countenances tend to mirror whatever we are looking at. The Lord is the source of light. If we look to Him, we will reflect His light; we will be, like the people David describes, "radiant." But if we focus our attention on things dark and gloomy and discouraging, that is how we will appear to others.

The lesson David communicates is twofold. First, let the Lord dispel your fear and gloom with the light of His countenance. Then become a reflector of His light to the world around you.

Faith's Response

Dispel my fear, Lord, with the light of Your countenance, and help me to reflect that light to others.

The Unseen Army

The angel of the LORD encamps around those
who fear Him,
And rescues them.

Psalm 34:7 NASB

For He will give His angels charge concerning
you,
To guard you in all your ways.

Psalm 91:11 NASB

Do you believe in angels? I do! I believe there are
myriads and myriads of good angels who are given
charge over God's people. The writer of Hebrews
tells us that all angels are "ministering spirits sent
to serve those who will inherit salvation" (Hebrews
1:14). I am glad to know that wherever I go, there
is an angel of God that encamps around me, ready
to rescue me.

In 2 Kings 6 we read that the prophet Elisha was
in a city besieged by a large alien army sent to capture him. His servant was dismayed by the tremendous numbers of the besieging army. But Elisha

Through the Psalms

replied, "Those who are with us are more than those who are with them." Then he prayed, "Lord, open his eyes so he may see." When the young man looked again, he saw the hills "full of horses and chariots of fire all around Elisha." Why around Elisha? Because Elisha fulfilled the qualification for such angelic protection: *He feared the Lord.*

That one man, Elisha, was the focus of heaven's armies. They protected not only the prophet himself. They were a defense for the young man with him and for all the people in the besieged city.

If God would but open our eyes, I believe we would see that the same is true today. "Those who are with us are more than those who are with them." We have a great unseen army on our side. Let us be encouraged. Let us take heart. Let us reckon with the presence of the Lord's angels encamped around us, ready to rescue us.

Faith's Response

Lord, please make the presence of Your unseen armies a living reality for me today.

Shielded

Contend, O Lᴏʀᴅ, with those who contend with
  me;
  fight against those who fight against me.
Take up shield and buckler;
  arise and come to my aid.
Brandish spear and block the way*
  against those who pursue me.
Say to my soul,
  "I am your salvation."

Psalm 35:1–3

*Alternative marginal translation

That was a prayer of David in a time of deep distress. He found himself surrounded by enemies pressing in against him and he saw no way to keep them out. He had exhausted his own strength and his own resources. So he cried out to the Lord: "Take Your stand against my enemies. Interpose Yourself between me and them." David saw that he needed more than weapons; he needed God in His own Person to be his defense.

David's prayer was answered at the time in a way that met his immediate need, but that was not the end. The final, conclusive answer to David's prayer came a thousand years later through David's greater Son, the Lord Jesus Christ. On the cross Jesus did just what David had cried out for. Jesus interposed Himself; He blocked the way against every enemy of our souls. By His atoning death He canceled every claim and silenced every accusation of Satan. He set a limit to Satan's territory. He created a boundary that Satan cannot pass over.

If you find yourself, like David, harassed by enemies of your soul too strong and cunning for you, then accept for yourself the answer to David's prayer. Take refuge behind the cross of Jesus, and hear Him say to your soul, "I am your salvation."

Faith's Response

Lord Jesus, by faith I see You now, crucified, blocking the way against every enemy of my soul.

Sharing God's Pleasures

How precious is Your lovingkindness, O God!
And the children of men take refuge in the
    shadow of Your wings.
They feast on the abundance of [Your] house;
And You give them to drink of the river of Your
    delights.

Psalm 36:7–8 NASB/NIV

What a beautiful picture of God's graciousness and goodness! First of all we turn to Him out of our need. We come to Him for refuge because we are oppressed, because we cannot handle our problems. We take refuge in the shadow of His wings. But once we are there under His shadow, we discover that He has provided much more for us than mere refuge. He has provided a feast. He has provided abundance. We feast on the abundance of His house.

Not only that, but He gives us to drink of "the river of His delights." Notice carefully what that implies. God does not give us to drink of a river of our own delights, but of His delights. He shares with us the things that delight Him. There is a great

difference between the things that delight us and the things that delight God. The things that delight God are pure, uplifting, edifying, totally good. On the other hand, there are many things that our carnal nature craves that are harmful. An obvious example is the habit of smoking. Many people find pleasure in smoking, yet we all know today that it is extremely harmful—a potential cause of cancer and heart disease.

God's pleasures are never like that. They are solely and totally good. They have no harmful after-effects. The deeper we drink of them, the greater the good they do us.

God invites us to share His abundance and His delights. What a tragedy it would be to reject His invitation and cling to pleasures that gratify our carnal nature, but are ultimately harmful! Let us cultivate a taste for the things that delight God!

Faith's Response

Lord, I ask You to purify my taste, so that I may enjoy the things You enjoy.

Delighted in God

Delight yourself in the Lord
  and he will give you the desires of your heart.

Psalm 37:4

Notice that first phrase: "Delight yourself." I once heard someone ask this question: "Do you enjoy your religion, or do you endure it?" To the majority of people, religion is something to endure, a kind of painful duty. However, that is not how God wants us to experience Him. The Westminster Confession, the basic doctrinal statement of the Presbyterian Church, says: "The supreme duty of man is to glorify God, and to *enjoy* Him forever." Have you ever thought of enjoying God?

God says, "Delight yourself in Me, and I will give you the desires of your heart." That does not mean simply that God will do for us everything that we might wish or think. The desires of our own carnal, unregenerate nature are often warped and perverted.

If God were to satisfy these desires, the final outcome would do us more harm than good. In their

place, however, God promises new desires, godly desires, beneficial desires—the kind of desires God Himself has. Then He will satisfy these desires, because they are the ones that He Himself has given us.

But first, David tells us, we must learn to delight ourselves in the Lord. This means that our personal relationship with the Lord becomes the most important thing in our lives. It takes precedence over all other relationships and over all other forms of satisfaction. There can be no "ulterior motives." We relate to God for His own sake, not for the sake of what we hope to receive from Him.

Then comes the paradox: This single-minded relationship to God for His own sake opens the way into a realm of satisfaction we could never otherwise envisage, much less enjoy.

Faith's Response

I will find my delight in God and seek no other source of satisfaction apart from Him.

Commit—Then Trust!

Commit your way to the LORD,
Trust also in Him, and He will do it.

Psalm 37:5 NASB

Do you want God in charge of your situation, your problems, your whole life? There are three simple steps that lead to this.

First, *commit* your way to the Lord. That is a single decisive act. Committing your way to the Lord is like depositing money in a bank. You hand your money over to the teller, take your own hands off it, and obtain a receipt for it. After that, you know that you have deposited your money in the bank. The receipt is your evidence.

Second, *trust* also in the Lord. Commitment is a single act, but trust is a continuing attitude. Once you have deposited your money in the bank, you do not go on worrying whether it is still there, or whether the bank knows what to do with it. You just trust the bank. In this case, however, you are not trusting the bank, you are trusting the Lord.

Through the Psalm

Once you have taken the first two steps, then the third step is the Lord's. *He will do it*. He will "bring it to pass" (KJV).

Whatever situation you have in mind, whatever need, whatever problem, whatever decision, commit it to the Lord—that is the *act*. From then on you go on trusting Him—that is the *attitude*. This gives you the wonderful, peaceful assurance that the Lord *will do it*. He is in control. You can trust the bank with your money and you can trust the Lord with your problem. Just take it to Him, commit it to Him, and continue trusting Him.

What about the receipt? That is the witness of the Holy Spirit within your heart that God has accepted your commitment.

Faith's Response

By a decision of my will, Lord, I commit to You that particular situation that concerns me and I trust You to work it out.

Open My Ears!

> Sacrifice and meal offering You have not
>   desired;
> My ears You have opened;
> Burnt offering and sin offering You have not
>   required.
> Then I said, "Behold, I come;
> In the scroll of the book it is written of me;
> I delight to do Your will, O my God. . . ."

Psalm 40:6–8 NASB

When David refers to burnt offering and meal offering and sin offering, he is speaking about the externals of religion. He is saying, in essence, that these by themselves are not sufficient. We may attend to all the externals, yet miss the part that really matters. He continues, "My ears You have opened." Here is the inner essence of true religion, which alone gives meaning to the externals. We need to hear the voice of God, speaking to us directly and personally. For this, God Himself must open our ears.

Only then will we be able to respond like the psalmist: "Behold, I come; in the scroll of the book it is written of me. . . ." When God opens our ears and we in turn surrender our lives to Him, we make the amazing and glorious discovery that He has a special plan for each one of us—a plan written from eternity "in the scroll of the book." The plans that God has for His people are infinitely varied. He never makes one person a carbon copy of another. His plan for each life is uniquely suited to all that is special and individual in each of us.

Without this revelation of God's individual will for us, we may find the mere externals of religion irksome and deadening. But when our ears are opened, then it becomes easy to say, "I delight to do Your will, O my God."

Faith's Response

Open my ears to hear, O Lord, and my eyes to see what is written in the scroll for my life.

Soul Thirst

As the deer pants for streams of water,
   so my soul pants for you, O God.
My soul thirsts for God, for the living God.
   When can I go and meet with God?

Psalm 42:1–2

I suppose we are all familiar with thirst in our personal experience. For me, the word evokes vivid pictures of three years in World War II spent with the British Army in the barren, dusty deserts of North Africa. At times our supply of water would be depleted and then, I recall, my whole being formed itself into a single insistent but inarticulate cry—for water! Nothing but water could silence that cry.

David speaks here of a different kind of thirst— a thirst not of the body, but of the soul. This, too, is no less vivid for me. I recall long years spent in the pursuit of satisfaction that always eluded me. I sought it in every form in which it presented itself to me—physical, aesthetic, intellectual—in music, drama, philosophy, travel, sensual indulgence. Yet the more earnestly I searched, the emptier and more frustrated I became.

Eventually I found the answer—the same answer David had found three thousand years earlier: "When can I go and meet with God?" There is a thirst of the soul, a deep inner longing of man's whole being, that cannot be satisfied with anything less than God Himself.

Perhaps you, too, have tried many sources, but have come away still unsatisfied. If so, it is important for you to understand two things: first, that nothing but God Himself will ever satisfy you; and second, that He is waiting to meet with you.

Faith's Response

O God, draw me to the place where I can meet with You and satisfy my soul's thirst.

The Release of Joy

Then I will go to the altar of God,
To God my exceeding joy. . . .

Psalm 43:4 NASB

David had learned two things concerning joy. First, there is only one source of joy: It is God Himself. Second, there is only one place where we can draw from that source: It is the altar. The altar is the place of sacrifice, the place of commitment and consecration, the place where our lives are laid down. Through the sacrifice we make at the altar, the joy that comes from God alone is released within us.

There is a great difference between joy and happiness. Joy is in the realm of the spirit. Happiness is in the realm of the soul. Happiness is related to our emotions, our feelings, our circumstances. When things are going well, we have happiness. When things are not going well, we have unhappiness. It is good to have happiness, but we cannot have it all the time.

Joy, on the other hand, is not dependent on feelings or circumstances. It does not depend on our physical condition. It is within the spirit. There is only one source of joy, and that is God—God Himself. God is eternal, unchangeable. That is why it is possible to have joy even when we cannot feel happiness or pleasure. Joy comes directly from God Himself. Just like God, joy is eternal, unchangeable, unaffected by situations or circumstances.

But joy is released only at the altar. We have to make up our minds, as David did, that we will go to God, to the altar—the place of sacrifice—the place of commitment and consecration—the place where we yield ourselves without reservation to God. Then we can have joy all the time, unchangeably.

Faith's Response

On Your altar, Lord, I lay down my life without reservation. Release within me the joy that comes from You alone.

The Beauty
of Righteousness

Your throne, O God, will last for ever and ever;
    a scepter of justice will be the scepter of your
    kingdom.
You love righteousness and hate wickedness;
    therefore God, your God, has set you above
    your companions
    by anointing you with the oil of joy.
All your robes are fragrant with myrrh and
    aloes and cassia;
    from palaces adorned with ivory
    the music of the strings makes you glad.

Psalm 45:6–8

The psalmist here gives us a prophetic picture of the Messiah—one that found its fulfillment in the Lord Jesus. The picture reveals the character of Jesus, His attitude in moral matters, and the reason why God exalted Him. It is important to understand that Jesus was not treated as a favored Son. He earned His promotion. The psalmist gives the reason: "You love righteousness and hate wickedness; *therefore*, God has set you above your companions. . . ." It was the attitude of Jesus in the matters of righteousness and wickedness that caused God to promote Him. There is no neutrality in these matters. The righteousness that God approves leaves no room for compromise with wickedness.

This uncompromising righteousness is crowned with joy that comes from the anointing of the Holy Spirit. John the Baptist testified of Jesus: "I saw the Spirit come down from heaven as a dove and remain on him" (John 1:32). What marked Jesus as Messiah was that the Holy Spirit *remained* on Him. Never by word or deed did He give the dove cause to leave Him.

Such righteousness is adorned by beauty, too—garments permeated with fragrant spices and the melody of strings proceeding out of a palace adorned with ivory.

Contemplating such purity and loveliness, we echo the words of the Bride: "He is wholly desirable. . . . This is my beloved" (Song of Songs 5:16 NASB).

Faith's Response

Lord, anoint my eyes to see the beauty of true righteousness.

"Be Still, and Know"

> Nations are in uproar, kingdoms fall;
>> he [God] lifts his voice, the earth melts. . . .
> He makes wars cease to the ends of the earth;
>> he breaks the bow and shatters the spear,
>> he burns the shields with fire.
> "Be still, and know that I am God;
>> I will be exalted among the nations,
>> I will be exalted in the earth."

Psalm 46:6, 9–10

The psalmist describes a scene of worldwide confusion. Nations are in an uproar; kingdoms are falling. There is a clash of weapons; war is imminent. Then, in the midst of it all, God intervenes. He brings all the frenzied activity of the nations to a standstill. To His own people He says: "Be still, and know that I am God."

The scene today answers exactly to the psalmist's prophetic picture: nations in an uproar; kingdoms falling; accelerating accumulation of armaments; ever-present threat of war. In the midst of all this we must listen to what God is saying to His people: "Be still . . . be still, and know . . ."

Through the Psalms

We dare not permit the confusion in the world around us to disturb our own spirits. No matter how great the pressures, we must continually cultivate an inner stillness that permits us to hear what God is saying. He is telling us: "I have foreknown all that you see around you. I am not unprepared. When all My purposes have ripened, I will intervene. Do not give way to fear. The situation is not out of control. Ultimately all will work out for My glory and for your good."

In His last great prophetic discourse, Jesus gave a similar picture of the world at the close of the present age, but He added: "When these things begin to take place, stand up and lift up your heads, because your redemption is drawing near" (Luke 21:28).

Faith's Response

Help me, Lord, to maintain an inner stillness so that I can hear Your voice in spite of all the confusion around me.

The Way Out Is Up

"Sacrifice thank offerings to God,
    fulfill your vows to the Most High,
and call upon me in the day of trouble;
    I will deliver you, and you will honor me."

Psalm 50:14–15

Here is the divine way out of trouble. Just now you may be in the midst of it. Everything is going against you, and you cannot see any way out. But listen to what the psalmist says: The way *out* is *up*—to God. "Sacrifice thank offerings. . . ." That sounds senseless, but try it anyway! In the midst of all your problems, stop worrying and start thanking God. Lift your voice to God—not in complaining, but in praise. Offer Him a sacrifice of thanksgiving.

A sacrifice always costs you something. To start thanking God in such a situation goes against the grain. But it is a sacrifice that pleases God. In return, God promises: "When you offer Me your sacrifice of thankfulness in the midst of all the trouble, then I will intervene on your behalf. I will deliver you and you will honor Me."

In the last verse of the psalm God returns to this theme. He says: "He who sacrifices thank offerings honors me, and he prepares the way so that I may show him the salvation of God." God is waiting to deliver you. But He requires you to prepare the way for Him to intervene in your situation. This you do when you begin to sacrifice your thank offerings to Him.

In Philippi Paul and Silas were in the "maximum security" section of the jail. Their feet were fastened in the stocks, their backs bleeding from a savage beating. Nevertheless, at midnight—the darkest hour—they were praying and singing hymns. Suddenly God intervened with an earthquake. They were instantly released and the jailer converted (Acts 16:22–34). It was their sacrifice of praise that had prepared the way for God's intervention.

Faith's Response

Right now, Lord, in the midst of my trouble, I offer to You my sacrifices of praise and thankfulness.

The Secret
Hidden Wisdom

Behold, thou desirest truth in the inward parts:
and in the hidden part thou shalt make me to
know wisdom.

Psalm 51:6 KJV

The introductory word *behold* indicates a sudden
awareness of truth never previously perceived.
What is it that God really looks for in our lives?
First and foremost, it is not the external practices
of religion that earn us a reputation for piety with
our fellow men. God looks much deeper than that.
He looks right down into the innermost depths of
our hearts. "The LORD does not look at the things
man looks at. Man looks at the outward appear-
ance, but the LORD looks at the heart" (1 Samuel
16:7).

God desires "truth in the inward parts." That is
the very opposite of religious externalism. Our fellow human beings may perhaps be impressed or
deceived by this, but not God! He looks below all
that; He looks for inner honesty and sincerity. It is

here that each of us needs to examine himself: Am I truly open with God? Am I transparent in my relationship with Him? Do the words I speak really express what I feel in my heart?

When we come to this state of inner transparency before God, we enter the second phase of the truth that David apprehended: "In the hidden part thou shalt make me to know wisdom." There is a "hidden wisdom of God," designed for the "hidden part" of man, which can be received only by those whose hearts are totally and unreservedly open to God.

Paul tells us that the ability to receive this wisdom is the mark of true spiritual maturity: "Yet among the mature we do impart wisdom . . . a secret and hidden wisdom of God, which God decreed before the ages for our glorification" (1 Corinthians 2:6–7 RSV).

Faith's Response

I renounce all insincerity and empty formalism, that I may learn God's hidden wisdom.

A Pure Heart

Create in me a pure heart, O God,
    and renew a steadfast spirit within me.

Psalm 51:10

There are some things man can do and some that
he cannot. Man can make things. He can manu-
facture, adjust, adapt, repair. But one thing man
cannot do is *create.* Only God is the Creator.

At this point in his life, David had been brought
face-to-face with the reality of his own sinfulness.
Confronted by the prophet Nathan concerning his
adultery with Bathsheba, he glimpsed—perhaps
for the first time in his life—the true condition of
his own heart. He saw the devastation that had
been wrought there by sin and realized that there
was nothing he could do. He could not adjust. He
could not repair. He could not reform. All of that
was totally inadequate. And so, in agony of soul,
he turned to God and asked God to do what He
alone could do—to *create* in him a pure heart.

If you and I could see into our own hearts as
David saw into his, we would each recognize the

same condition. The effects of sin have been so disastrous that we have no remedy. It is no good trying to repair, to adapt, to reform. There is only one remedy left to us. We can do as David did. We can acknowledge the depth of our need and then turn to God with this prayer: "God, I cannot change myself. I cannot reform myself. My heart is corrupted and sinful. Do for me what I cannot do for myself. Create in me a pure heart, O God."

The final, universal answer to David's cry was provided by the sacrifice of Jesus. Through this, the miracle of a new creation is made available to all humanity.

"Therefore, if anyone is in Christ, he is a new creation; the old has gone, the new has come!" (2 Corinthians 5:17).

Faith's Response

O God of David and of Jesus, create in me, too, a pure heart!

A Broken Spirit

You do not delight in sacrifice, or I would bring
   it;
     you do not take pleasure in burnt offerings.
The sacrifices of God are a broken spirit;
     a broken and contrite heart,
     O God, you will not despise.

Psalm 51:16–17

Through his own personal agony, David has come
to a new understanding of what it is that God really
requires from man. First, God is not interested in
externals—represented here by "offerings" and
"sacrifices." This does not necessarily mean that
God never requires any external observances of
religion. Many other passages of Scripture indicate that at times He does. But it means that these
are not the things He requires first and foremost.
If our religion contains nothing more than such
external observances, then God takes no pleasure
in them.

    Always, God looks below the externals. He looks
to the motives and to the attitude of the heart.
What does He look for there? "A broken spirit,"

David tells us, "a broken and contrite heart." These are strange words to our ears these days. What does it mean that God desires a broken spirit? Does He want to beat us down and humiliate us? No, I am sure that is not His purpose.

What, then, is a broken spirit? I believe it is a spirit that has come totally to the end of itself. It makes no claims, offers no arguments. All independence, all self-will, all self-righteousness have been purged out. Such a spirit turns simply and solely to God, trusting not in its own merits, but only in God's infinite and unmerited mercy.

If we will permit Him, God knows how to produce this brokenness of spirit in each of us. He treats each of us as individuals. He never violates our personality. He uses only the precise degree of pressure needed to achieve His end.

"For he does not willingly bring affliction or grief to the children of men" (Lamentations 3:33).

Faith's Response

Lord, do whatever is needed in my heart and life so that I can offer You sacrifices that please You.

How to Overcome Fear

When I am afraid,
   I will trust in you.
In God, whose word I praise,
   in God I trust; I will not be afraid.

Psalm 56:3–4

One thing I especially appreciate in the Bible is its honesty. It faces facts. It pictures life as it is. It takes account of human weakness. David does not make false claims for himself. He does not say, "I will never be afraid." Rather, he acknowledges: "There may come times when I will be afraid. But when those times come, I will know what to do. I will trust in God and I will praise His word—His sure, unfailing word. Trusting and praising will overcome my fear."

In the life of faith there is often a conflict between two areas of our being: our spirit and our emotions. In our emotions we go through all the reactions of fear, perhaps even of panic. In vain we struggle against it. It grips us. But there is another area of our being—the spirit—that will

not yield to panic, that does not accept the dictates of emotions. The spirit within us says, "I will not accept the verdict of my emotions about this situation. I will turn to God. I will remember what His Word says. I will find the promise of God that meets my need. In my emotions I may feel fear, but in my innermost being I trust, and that trust imparts to me a security and a confidence that are much deeper than my emotions."

In such a situation our personality may be compared to a river on a windy day. Our emotions are like the waves on the surface—troubled and tossed. But in the innermost depths of our being, the life of our spirit flows on in untroubled peace.

Faith's Response

Lord, I thank You for the peace deep inside me that is not affected by the winds on life's surface.

A Bottle Full of Tears

You have taken account of my wanderings;
Put my tears in Your bottle;
Are they not in Your book?

Psalm 56:8 NASB

This is the cry of a desperate soul—someone who knows what it is to be a wanderer, a fugitive, an exile; someone who knows what it is to shed many tears. Yet even in his tears and in his exile, he finds comfort. He realizes that the eye of God is upon him. God is taking note of everything he goes through. A record is being kept in God's book of all that he suffers for righteousness' sake.

Even his tears are not shed in vain. They are tears of grief and loneliness, but not of despair. There is a future to them. At present they are tokens of suffering, but one day each tear will become the theme for a song of praise. So the exile says to God, "Put my tears in Thy bottle—store them up carefully for me." He does not want to lose the theme for even one song.

Suffering is an almost inevitable part of human life, but it is not necessarily evil. Its outcome will

depend on how we respond to it. There is a French proverb that says: "To be beautiful one must suffer." Suffering endured in faith and for the sake of righteousness imparts a unique beauty that death cannot destroy.

So do not squander your sufferings! Make sure they are stored for eternity. They will be transformed into a corresponding glory.

"I consider that our present sufferings are not worth comparing with the glory that will be revealed in us" (Romans 8:18).

Faith's Response

Lord Jesus, help me to see my sufferings in the light of eternity.

From the Ends
of the Earth

Hear my cry, O God;
   listen to my prayer.
From the ends of the earth I call to you,
   I call as my heart grows faint. . . .

Psalm 61:1–2

Those words have a very special meaning for me. They were given to me by the Holy Spirit during a period of crisis in my life and at a very precise time and place. I was facing great personal disappointment and sorrow. It seemed indeed that the waves and billows of God were going over my soul. I was on my way from the United States to hold a series of meetings in Australia. Seated in a jet airplane six miles above the Pacific, I opened my Bible at random to the words, "From the ends of the earth I call to you." I thought to myself, "That's remarkable. That's exactly where I'm headed—the ends of the earth." (Australia is in the area of the earth farthest from the place where the psalmist wrote these words.) Then I asked myself, "Why am I going there? What is God's purpose?"

I read the verse through again: "From the ends of the earth I call to you, I call as my heart grows faint." I realized that in His infinite wisdom God was taking me all that long journey, not merely to preach to others, but, even more important, to give myself to prayer in a situation where I was separated by thousands of miles from the immediate pressures of my problem—where I could wait upon God without distraction.

There came a special week when I spent the greater part of each day in prayer. As I called to God from the ends of the earth, He sovereignly intervened in my situation. By the time I returned to the United States, every problem had been resolved, every barrier removed. The way was open for me to move forward in God's plan for my life.

Faith's Response

Do You have a prayer appointment with me, Lord, that You are waiting for me to keep?

In God Alone

My soul finds rest in God alone;
   my salvation comes from him.
He alone is my rock and my salvation;
   he is my fortress, I will never be shaken. . . .
Find rest, O my soul, in God alone;
   my hope comes from him.
He alone is my rock and my salvation;
   he is my fortress, I will not be shaken.

Psalm 62:1–2, 5–6

There is one very important word that occurs four times in succession in these verses—once in each verse. The word is *alone*. The psalmist enumerates a series of infinitely precious blessings that come only from God Himself. First and foremost among these blessings is salvation. Closely associated are also: rest; strength (the rock); protection (the fortress); and hope. In a sense these last four blessings are all byproducts of the first—that is, salvation.

The only ultimate source of salvation is God Himself—God alone. We dare not suggest that God is insufficient and that something further is necessary beyond God Himself. Salvation does not

Through the Psalm

depend on God plus the Law, or God plus the Church—or God plus anything else. It depends on God alone.

The prophet Isaiah is another witness to the absolute uniqueness and all-sufficiency of God for salvation. Out of his own experience he declares: "Surely God is my salvation. . . . The LORD, the LORD, is my strength and my song; he has become my salvation" (Isaiah 12:2).

There are two opposite errors into which we may fall. On the one hand, if we suggest that salvation depends on something *more* than God, we dishonor Him and discredit His all-sufficiency. On the other hand, if we look for salvation in anything *less* than God, we will look in vain.

But when God Himself becomes our salvation, then the other associated blessings follow: rest, strength, protection and hope.

Faith's Response

Find rest, O my soul, in God alone; my salvation comes from Him.

Encounter with God

O God, you are my God,
   earnestly I seek you;
my soul thirsts for you,
   my body longs for you,
in a dry and weary land
   where there is no water.
I have seen you in the sanctuary
   and beheld your power and your glory. . . .
On my bed I remember you;
   I think of you through the watches of the
   night.

Psalm 63:1–2, 6

How important it is to have your own personal revelation of God! Not just to rely on what somebody else has told you, or what you have read in a book, or even what you have heard in church. All that may be good, but it is not sufficient. There must come a time when you experience God for yourself—when you come to know Him firsthand, when you have such a revelation of God that nothing less than God Himself can ever fully satisfy you.

David had that kind of revelation. He says to God, "I have seen You in the sanctuary; I have beheld Your power and Your glory. And now I am in a dry and thirsty land, but my soul longs for You more than it does for water. Even when I lie in bed at night, my meditation is of You. You fill my heart and my mind, my imagination, my longing. All the day through I am taken up with You, my God. There is no other source of true satisfaction. My soul does not find rest in any other way. I have seen You and I have known You in a way I can never forget. It has forever determined the course of my life."

Do you wonder whether such an experience is possible today? Let me assure you, out of personal experience, that it is. One night in 1941, in a barracks room of the British Army, I met God revealed in Jesus Christ. That encounter totally and permanently transformed my life. Today, more than sixty years later, I have the same intense thirst in my soul that David describes—a thirst that can be satisfied by nothing less than God Himself.

Faith's Response

O God, fill my whole being, I pray, with the revelation of Yourself!

God Hears and Answers

Praise awaits you, O God, in Zion;
　　to you our vows will be fulfilled.
O you who hear prayer,
　　to you all men will come.
When we were overwhelmed by sins,
　　you forgave for our transgressions.

Psalm 65:1–3

It often happens that in a counseling session with some troubled soul—someone, perhaps, who is struggling with a broken marriage or a total breakdown of their health—I have to tell that person very honestly, "I don't have the answer to your problem. I can't tell you exactly what to do. But one thing I can tell you: God hears and answers prayer."

That is just what the psalmist says here: "O you who hear prayer, to you all men will come." Somewhere in the life of every one of us there is a crossroads where we come face-to-face with our need of God. Then the thing that matters most is to know that God responds to prayer. Ultimately, that is what will bring the whole of humanity to God—the fact that He hears and answers prayer.

Above all others, there is one special prayer that God delights to answer, and that is the prayer for forgiveness of our sins. When we have sinned and failed God and man, we do not need to turn away in despair. So often the enemy of our souls would seek to convince us that there is no use in praying; we have gone too far, or sunk too low. But that is not true! God still waits to hear our prayer. If we cry to Him for forgiveness, He will answer. Then we will be able to say, with David: "When we were overwhelmed by sins, you atoned for our transgressions."

Never let fear or guilt or despair keep you from praying. Remember, in the depths of your agony: God hears, and He answers prayer.

Faith's Response

Lord, I have exhausted every human solution, but I still believe You will answer my prayer.

Refined in the Furnace

For you, O God, tested us;
    you refined us like silver.

Psalm 66:10

One thing the Bible teaches clearly is that God tests His people. If we wish to belong to the people of God, then we must be prepared to be tested. One vivid picture of the way God tests us, used many times in Scripture, is that of a metalworker purifying silver.

In Bible times such a man would place the silver in a metal container over the hottest possible fire. Then, as the silver began to melt and bubble in the heat, the impurities would rise to the surface in the form of a scum, known as "dross," and the metal worker would skim them off. He would patiently continue this process of skimming until there was no impurity left in the silver. The final test of purity would come when the metalworker, peering into the silver, could see his own face mirrored there without distortion. Then he would know that all the dross had been removed.

That is just how God tests us—but the furnace He uses is affliction. The hotter the furnace, the more quickly the impurities are brought to the surface. Gently and patiently, God skims them off with the invisible skimmer of His Holy Spirit. He goes on with the process until there are no more impurities and He sees His own image reflected in our lives. Then He knows that the process of refining has been successful, and He takes us out of the furnace.

"See, I have refined you, though not as silver; I have tested you in the furnace of affliction" (Isaiah 48:10).

Faith's Response

Lord, I do not ask to escape the testing, but for grace to endure it, until You are satisfied with my life.

Hope for the Lonely

God sets the lonely in families,
  he leads forth the prisoners with singing;
  but the rebellious live in a sun-scorched land.

Psalm 68:6

To be lonely is a very unhappy condition. Yet in today's world there are millions and millions of lonely people. Even though the population of the earth is increasing rapidly, and even though many people live in large cities, these large cities and this highly populated earth of ours are filled with lonely people.

It is possible to be lonely in the midst of a crowd. It is possible to be lonely in a big city. In fact, that is the worst form of loneliness—to be surrounded by people and yet cut off from them by an invisible barrier you do not know how to break through.

Yet loneliness is not God's plan for man's life. From eternity God is a Father. The source of all fatherhood—of every family—in heaven and on earth is God (Ephesians 3:14–15). Right at the beginning of human history God provided a mate

for the first man because He said it was not good for man to be alone. That is God's attitude. He wants to take us out of our loneliness and to set us in the family of God. He wants to give us brothers and sisters with whom to share His love.

There may be some special barrier in your life—whether of sin or of circumstances—that keeps you shut up in the prison of your loneliness. But if so, God is ready to deliver you and to lead you forth with singing.

There is just one kind of person whom God cannot help out of loneliness: the rebellious. Such a person must continue to live in a sun-scorched land. Rebelliousness is a barrier that a person raises by his own will, and he is the only one who can take it down. Until he does that, it will continue to shut him off from fellowship with both God and man.

Faith's Response

Lord, if it is rebelliousness that keeps me a lonely person, help me to take that barrier down.

Strength That Never Fails

My flesh and my heart may fail,
  but God is the strength of my heart
  and my portion forever.

Psalm 73:26

For those who walk by faith there is an ongoing tension between two kinds of life. One is visible and external, the other invisible and eternal. The external is fading; it is impermanent. But there is something inside every believer that is eternal—something from God that is linked directly to Him, something that does not fade or wither.

Paul writes on this tension from his own experience: "Therefore we do not lose heart, but though our outer man is decaying, yet our inner man is being renewed day by day. . . . For the things which are seen are temporal, but the things which are not seen are eternal" (2 Corinthians 4:16, 18 NASB).

These words always remind me of my first wife, Lydia. Toward the end of her life she suffered from a weak heart, yet she was an amazingly strong and active woman and continued so almost to her last

week on earth. At times she would feel her physical heart failing, but she would always say: "My flesh and my heart may fail, but God is the strength of my heart and my portion forever." From her I learned the lesson that we must not let the external dictate to the internal. Within the life committed to God, there is an inner source of strength not subject to the weaknesses and fluctuations of our physical body.

Eventually God called Lydia home in tremendous victory, after fifty years of active and fruitful Christian service. She left behind the testimony of a life that had demonstrated the supremacy of the internal over the external. She had learned how to keep her inner being linked to God, the real source of strength.

Faith's Response

God, help me to live in such a way that the temporal never dictates to the eternal.

Homesick

My soul yearns, even faints,
   for the courts of the Lord;
my heart and my flesh cry out
   for the living God.
Even the sparrow has found a home,
   and the swallow a nest for herself,
   where she may have her young—
a place near your altar,
   O Lord Almighty, my King and my God.
Blessed are those who dwell in your house;
   they are ever praising you.

                              Psalm 84:2–4

Every human soul longs for one thing: a home. A homeless person is an unhappy person—in fact, a lost person. The psalmist cries out in agony, "Lord, even the sparrow has found a home, the swallow a nest for herself. I need a home, too!"

The sparrow and the swallow whom the psalmist describes have set a pattern for every lost, confused soul. The place they have chosen for a home is near God's altar. This is the place where every human soul must ultimately find its home. On God's side, the altar represents propitiation for sin and recon-ciliation. On man's side, it represents surrender and commitment. Here is the home of the soul, where it finds true rest and peace.

In the great city of Glasgow in Scotland, there is a main intersection known as "the Cross." One day a tall British "bobby" on his beat found a small boy sitting in tears on the curb. "I'm lost," he told the policeman. "I can't find my way home."

"I'll have to take you to the station," the police-man said, and began to lead the boy by the hand. When they reached "the Cross," the boy looked around for a moment, then exclaimed, "I know the way from here!" Letting go of the policeman's hand, he ran off confidently toward his home.

So it is with the human soul that comes to the Cross. From there it can find the way home.

Faith's Response

Lord, like Your servant of old, I, too, am homesick. Help me to find that place near Your altar.

An Undivided Heart

Teach me your way, O Lᴏʀᴅ,
    and I will walk in your truth;
give me an undivided heart,
    that I may fear your name.
I will praise you, O Lᴏʀᴅ my God,
    with all my heart. . . .

Psalm 86:11–12

Do we truly desire success in our walk with God? Then we must give careful heed to these words of David, for he focuses on two essential requirements.

First, David reveals our need of teaching that can come only from God: "Teach me your way, O Lᴏʀᴅ, and I will walk in your truth." Left to ourselves, we can neither discern nor apply God's truth. We cannot walk in God's way unless He Himself in His mercy teaches us that way.

Second, David focuses on the attitude of heart needed to receive and apply God's teaching. In verse 11 he says, "Give me an undivided heart," and in verse 12 he continues, "I will praise you with all my heart." Twice he emphasizes the response of the heart: "An undivided heart . . . with all my heart . . ."

Here is the crucial issue: that we have an undivided heart. We can have no conflicting loyalty, no second option. All our springs must be in God; all our expectations must be from Him.

I have discovered in the life of faith that the further we go in God, the fewer our options. The way becomes narrower and narrower. Ultimately those who complete the course are those who have found their total satisfaction in God. It is not God plus something; it is God alone. Our heart is undivided when we do not look anywhere but to God for our satisfaction, our peace, our life.

Faith's Response

Lord, I renounce every claim on my heart's affection that conflicts with my loyalty to You.

At Home in Eternity

Before the mountains were born
    or you brought forth the earth and the world,
    from everlasting to everlasting you are
    God. . . .
For a thousand years in your sight
    are like a day that has just gone by,
    or like a watch in the night.

Psalm 90:2, 4

There is a difference between time and eternity—
a difference of kind, not merely of duration. The
mountains were born. The earth and the world
were brought forth. All that is in the past tense.
But when the psalmist turns to God he says, "From
everlasting to everlasting you *are* God." Not, "You
were God," but, "You *are* God." In God past, present and future all meet. He is and He was and He
is to come (Revelation 1:4).

God does not indwell time, He indwells eternity.
Eternity is not just a very long period of time; it is
a different mode of being. It is something from
another world, something higher than time. With

God it is always, "You are." His very name is I AM (Exodus 3:14).

From the serenity and heights of eternity God beholds time. From that viewpoint, a thousand years with God are just like a day that has gone by, or a watch in the night. The night in biblical times was divided into four watches of three hours each. So a thousand years with God is like three hours that have passed in our experience.

God invites each of us to know Him personally, and He thus opens a door for us out of time into eternity. In our physical being, we are still confined within the limits of time, but our spirits find their true dwelling place in eternity.

"Now this is eternal life: that they may know you, the only true God, and Jesus Christ, whom you have sent" (John 17:3).

Faith's Response

Lord, may my spirit be so at home with You in eternity that it will never be a prisoner of time.

Setting Right Priorities

Teach us to number our days aright,
that we may gain a heart of wisdom.

Psalm 90:12

What does that mean—to "number our days aright"? Permit me to follow that up with another question: What is the thing in your life that you find hardest to manage—the thing you most often find yourself short of? Many people would probably be inclined to answer, Money. But in my experience there is something much harder to manage—something I am much more often short of. It is, Time! I find time is the hardest thing in life to manage properly. For this reason, the stewardship of time is the supreme test of our personal discipline and of the genuineness of our Christian commitment.

From my heart, therefore, I echo this prayer of the psalmist: *Teach me to number my days aright.* Practically, this means: Teach me to set my priorities in order. Teach me to give enough time to the

things that matter most. Only in this way can I "gain a heart of wisdom."

In the final analysis, our priorities of time indicate the real values that govern our lives. Things that have a low priority will probably drop off the bottom of the list. If we do not give high priority to things that really matter—such as prayer and Bible reading—our whole lives will be out of order. We may then be tempted to offer the excuse, "I didn't have enough time." But the real truth will be, "I didn't make right use of my time."

Before it is too late, join with me in praying, *Teach us to number our days aright.*

Faith's Response

Lord, I put my life before You as a blank sheet, and I ask You by Your Spirit to write upon it Your priorities for me.

Planted in God's House

The righteous will flourish like a palm tree,
   they will grow like a cedar of Lebanon;
planted in the house of the Lord,
   they will flourish in the courts of our God.
They will still bear fruit in old age,
   they will stay fresh and green,
proclaiming, "The Lord is upright;
   he is my Rock, and there is no wickedness in
   him."

Psalm 92:12–15

The life of a truly righteous man is here compared to two trees: a palm tree and a cedar. The essence of the palm tree is that it grows tall and upright, and its fruit is formed like a crown in the top of the tree. The longer it lives, the higher it grows and the more impressive its fruit becomes. The cedar, on the other hand, is the king of all trees, the most magnificent, the most majestic. Such is a righteous man in his maturity.

Both these pictures of righteousness, however, apply only to those who are "planted in the house of the Lord." The word *planted* is important. It speaks of enduring commitment. Someone has popularized the prayer: *Lord, help me to bloom where I am planted.*

Unfortunately, some Christians are never willing to be planted anywhere. They are always busy but never truly committed. They never put down roots, so they never bring forth fruit. Only those willing to be planted will bear enduring fruit. These are the ones who continue to bear fruit in old age. They become a visible testimony to God's faithfulness. Their very lives proclaim, "The LORD is upright . . . and there is no wickedness in him."

If you want to understand the nature of the Lord, look at the life of a righteous man in his maturity, and you will see the Lord's faithfulness mirrored there.

Faith's Response

I renounce the glamour of the temporary, and I am willing to make the commitment that alone produces enduring fruit.

Blessed Discipline

> Blessed is the man you discipline, O LORD,
>   the man you teach from your law;
> you grant him relief from days of trouble,
>   till a pit is dug for the wicked.

> Psalm 94:12–13

God is the first and the greatest of all educational psychologists. For a number of years I was principal of a teacher training college. Through my observations at that time, I came to appreciate in a new way the psychological principles of Scripture in the field of teaching. The psalmist here puts the Lord's *discipline* before his *teaching,* and thus establishes one great basic principle: *Without discipline there can be no real teaching.*

Herein lies a common problem of many contemporary educational systems: discipline has been abandoned, and with it teaching has ceased. I know from my own experience that if a teacher cannot exercise discipline, he cannot really teach. God, however, is wiser than that. He never tries to teach those who refuse His discipline.

The psalmist goes on to reveal a wonderful reward for the man who comes under God's discipline and accepts His teaching: "You grant him relief from days of trouble, till a pit is dug for the wicked." In the secret processes of history, God is digging a pit for the wicked; He is preparing a season of judgment and retribution. He has committed Himself, however, to spare those who have submitted to His discipline and teaching.

We are thus confronted with two alternatives: We can come under God's discipline now and be preserved from His judgment; or we can refuse God's discipline now and come under His judgment in the days ahead.

Faith's Response

I gladly submit to Your discipline now, Lord, and I trust You to preserve me from the days of trouble ahead.

When My Foot Slips

When I said, "My foot is slipping,"
  your love, O LORD, supported me.
When anxiety was great within me,
  your consolation brought joy to my soul.

Psalm 94:18–19

There is one thing that especially attracts me about the Bible's picture of God: He is so understanding. He knows our weaknesses, but He does not reject us on account of them. He does not ask us to present to Him, or to the world, a façade of strength that has no basis in reality. All He asks is that we sincerely yield to Him all that we have, no matter how inadequate it may seem. Beyond that, His grace supplies.

"My foot is slipping," the psalmist cried out. He was on the verge of falling and could not save himself. But the moment he acknowledged his need, God came to his rescue: "Your love, O LORD, supported me." Here is a pattern for each of us to remember. When our foot begins to slip and we have lost control, God does not ask us to try to save ourselves. We have only to voice our need to Him and His love will be there, supporting and upholding us.

In the next verse the psalmist describes his own inner reactions: "When anxiety was great within me, your consolation brought joy to my soul." It is in times of greatest anxiety that God suddenly floods our soul with His overwhelming joy. In fact, the greater the pressure we are under, the more wonderful is our experience of God's consolation.

In 2 Corinthians 1:8–9 Paul describes just such an experience: "We were under great pressure, far beyond our ability to endure, so that we despaired even of life. Indeed, in our hearts we felt the sentence of death. But this happened that we might not rely on ourselves but on God, who raises the dead."

Faith's Response

When my foot begins to slip, God, help me to remember that Your love is there to support me.

Access Through Worship

> Come, let us sing for joy to the LORD;
> > let us shout aloud to the Rock of our
> > salvation.
> Let us come before him with thanksgiving
> > and extol him with music and song. . . .
> Come, let us bow down in worship,
> > let us kneel before the LORD our Maker. . . .
> Today, if you hear his voice,
> > do not harden your hearts. . . .
>
> > > Psalm 95:1–2, 6, 7–8

There is a beautiful progression here that brings us into the immediate presence of God. It starts with loud and jubilant praise and thanksgiving: "Let us sing for joy . . . let us shout aloud . . ." God encourages us to express freely our praises and our thanksgiving. We all need the spiritual release that this gives.

Then, as we go further, the mood changes: "Come, let us bow down in worship, let us kneel before the LORD our Maker." Praise and thanksgiving lead us on to worship. Worship is not so much an utterance as an attitude. It is bowing down, kneeling—even at times prostrating ourselves before God. Every part of our being and every area of our personality is involved. All unite in total, unreserved submission to God.

When we come into this attitude of worship, we are able to hear God speaking directly to us. That is why the psalmist continues, "Today, if you hear his voice. . . ." This takes us beyond activities such as saying prayers or reading the Bible, important though these may be. It brings our spirits into direct communication with God.

The pathway that the psalmist here describes takes us through praise and thanksgiving into worship and stillness before God. It can bring us into a land of delight and abundance such as our natural minds could never envision, a land where "no eye has seen, no ear has heard, no mind has conceived what God has prepared for those who love him" (1 Corinthians 2:9).

Faith's Response

Lead me, Lord, along this path that brings me into Your immediate presence.

A New Song

Sing to the LORD a new song;
sing to the LORD, all the earth.

Psalm 96:1

The Psalms are full of exhortations to praise God in song. The one here quoted contains a special challenge. The Lord asks from us a *new* song. He never wants our praise of Him to become old or stale, or to degenerate into ritual and routine. How can we always be ready with a new song?

In Ephesians 5:18–19 Paul shows us the way: "Be filled with the Spirit, speaking to one another in psalms and hymns and spiritual songs, singing and making melody with your heart to the Lord" (NASB). Praise of the kind that the Lord requires and that Paul describes can come only from a heart supernaturally filled with the Holy Spirit. The infilling of the Holy Spirit is an indispensable prerequisite.

Out of the Spirit's fullness proceed three kinds of praise: psalms, hymns and spiritual songs. Psalms are those already recorded for us in the inspired words of Scripture. In the category of hymns belong the grand, familiar songs of the Church that express our common faith. But spiritual songs are not composed in advance. They are given spontaneously by the Holy Spirit. They are truly "new" songs.

Each time we enter God's presence in worship and catch a glimpse of His grace or glory that we have never seen before, the Holy Spirit gives us a new song appropriate to the new revelation. It may be in our own language or in one given by the Spirit. In either case, it is a spontaneous response to a fresh revelation of God. Thus our worship always continues to be as fresh as God's unfolding revelation of Himself.

Faith's Response

Holy Spirit, grant me songs to worship the Lord that are as fresh as His grace.

Awaiting the Climax

Let the heavens rejoice, let the earth be glad;
    let the sea resound, and all that is in it;
    let the fields be jubilant, and everything in
    them.
Then all the trees of the forest will sing for joy;
    they will sing before the LORD, for he comes,
    he comes to judge the earth.
He will judge the world in righteousness
    and the peoples in his truth.

Psalm 96:11–13

"The creation waits in eager expectation for the sons of God to be revealed. For the creation was subjected to frustration, not by its own choice . . ." (Romans 8:19–20). Man by his rebellion against his Creator brought corruption and decay upon the whole natural world around him. That which was blighted through his fall can be restored only through his redemption. This is the climax that all nature awaits. Too often man himself loses sight of this, but the anticipation of nature grows stronger all the time.

With insight given by the Holy Spirit, the psalmist here interprets the wordless longing of the natural world around him. In his spirit he senses a hushed anticipation, like the stillness in a concert auditorium as the conductor with upraised baton surveys his orchestra to make sure that each player is ready for the opening note. Heaven above and earth beneath, seas and fields and trees, all await the coming of the Lord to restore to them what was lost through man's fall. At that moment, like the orchestra as the baton descends, they will break forth into a symphony of praise and jubilation.

How about you and me? Are we as ready as nature is for that great climax? May God grant that you and I be more expectant and excited than the trees and the fields and the seas and the heavens!

Faith's Response

By Your Spirit, Lord, keep me in continual excited anticipation of Your coming.

Gates of Praise

Enter his gates with thanksgiving
and his courts with praise;
give thanks to him and praise his name.
For the Lord is good and his love endures
forever;
his faithfulness continues through all
generations.

Psalm 100:4–5

How important it is for each of us to know the way into God's presence! How do we enter His gates? How do we come into His courts? The psalmist points out the way that God has ordained: We enter His gates with thanksgiving, His courts with praise. It is only as we come to God with thanksgiving and with praise that we have access into His presence.

The prophet Isaiah likens the presence of God among His people to a city, concerning which he says: "You will call your walls Salvation and your gates Praise" (Isaiah 60:18). The only way through those walls of Salvation is by the gates of Praise.

Unless we learn to approach God with praise, we have no access into His presence.

Confronted with this requirement, we are sometimes tempted to look around us at our situation and ask: "But what do I have to thank God for? What do I have to praise Him for?" There may be nothing in our immediate circumstances that appears to give us cause to thank or praise God. It is just here that the psalmist comes to our help. He gives us three reasons to thank and praise that are not affected by our circumstances: first, the Lord is good; second, His love endures forever; third, His faithfulness continues through all generations. All three are eternal, unchanging facts. If we truly believe them, then we have no alternative but to praise God for them—continually!

Faith's Response

I believe in God's unchanging goodness, love and faithfulness, and I will never cease to praise Him for them.

The Appointed Time

My days are like the evening shadow;
   I wither away like grass.
But you, O Lord, sit enthroned forever;
   your renown endures through all
   generations.
You will arise and have compassion on Zion,
   for it is time to show favor to her;
   the appointed time has come. . . .
For the Lord will rebuild Zion
   and appear in his glory.

                              Psalm 102:11–13, 16

Here is a picture of a man in deep dejection and loneliness. He feels his life is ebbing away like the evening shadows and there is so little time left for him. He says, "I'm withering away like grass." Can you perhaps identify with him from some experience of your own? How would you respond?

The man pictured here made the right response. He looked away from himself and his own situation. By faith he lifted up his eyes to the Lord on His throne. He realized that the Lord does not

change with our circumstances. He is always on His throne. He never abdicates.

Out of this changed outlook came a prophetic revelation: The Lord has appointed a time to have compassion on His people and restore them to His favor. The Hebrew word translated *appointed time* is used to denote the fixed religious feasts of Israel's calendar—such as the Passover, Pentecost and Tabernacles. In the same way, on God's prophetic calendar there is set aside a specific period in human history for the restoration of Zion.

Today we have the unique privilege of living in the very time that the psalmist foresaw. How much more, then, should we respond as he did! Let us look away from our problems and anxieties. Let us look up to the Lord on His throne and realize that He is rebuilding Zion and preparing to appear in His glory.

Faith's Response

By faith I see You now, Lord, on Your throne and I know You are ready to have mercy.

Created to Praise

When the Lord shall build up Zion, he shall
    appear in his glory.
He will regard the prayer of the destitute, and
    not despise their prayer.
This shall be written for the generation to come:
    and the people which shall be created shall
    praise the Lord.

Psalm 102:16–18 KJV

The psalmist here points to one great sign that the
Lord's coming is near at hand: "When the Lord
shall build up Zion, he shall appear in his glory."
The rebuilding of Zion must precede and prepare
for the Lord's return in glory. That is precisely what
we see taking place today. The Lord is restoring
and rebuilding the nation of Israel. He is likewise
restoring and rebuilding the Christian Church. This
is one great evidence among many that the Lord
is ready to appear in His glory.

At this same period, the psalmist tells us, the
Lord will regard the prayer of the destitute. For so
long God's people have cried out to Him, and often
their cries seem to have gone unanswered. But a

day is coming when millions and millions of prayers will be answered in a short space of time by a single supreme intervention of God: the personal return of the Lord Jesus Christ.

The psalmist speaks also of this period as a unique generation, in which a people shall be created to praise the Lord. In this again he points to something we see taking place today: the restoration of praise. God's people have been so slack to praise Him for so many centuries that He is actually creating a people today for one specific purpose: that they may praise Him.

There is a logical theme that runs through all this. Once we understand what God is doing in this day for His people, our hearts must inevitably cry out for grace to respond with praise such as He deserves.

Faith's Response

Lord, let me be a part of the generation whose praise will welcome Your return.

Measureless Love

For as high as the heavens are above the earth,
   so great is his love for those who fear him;
as far as the east is from the west,
   so far has he removed our transgressions
   from us.

Psalm 103:11–12

David was neither an astronomer nor a geographer, but he was certainly inspired by the Holy Spirit. Searching for some standard of measurement to express the magnitude of God's love, he compares it to the height of the heavens. Today we are in a better position to grasp the significance of these words than David was when he wrote them. Astronomers have told us about countless millions of galaxies, all far greater than the galaxy of which our sun is a part. The facts they have given are such that no human intellect can remotely comprehend them. So it is with the love of God. Over and above that which our finite minds can absorb, there remains a vastness beyond our power to imagine.

David goes on to picture the way God deals with our guilt: "As far as the east is from the west, so far has he removed our transgressions from us." How thankful we should be that David did not use as his standard the distance from north to south! That is a finite, measurable distance. But the distance from east to west is infinite. No matter how far eastward we may go, there is still just as far to go as when we started. If we reverse our direction and go westward, the same is true.

That is how God deals with our guilt once He has forgiven us. He removes it so far from us that we can never again come near it. How foolish it would be on our part, then, to be troubled or condemned by what God Himself has placed forever beyond our reach!

Faith's Response

I accept God's love in all its vastness and His forgiveness in all its totality.

Tested by God's Promise

> He [God] sent a man before them,
> Joseph, who was sold as a slave.
> They afflicted his feet with fetters;
> He himself was laid in irons;
> Until the time that his word came to pass,
> The word of the LORD tested him.

Psalm 105:17–19 NASB

The life of Joseph began with great promise. Early in his youth the Lord gave him a dream, which showed him that he would be elevated to a position of great authority. He was to rule over his brothers. Even his father and mother would come bowing down before him. What happened next? The very opposite of what God had promised. His brothers betrayed him and sold him as a slave into Egypt. There, because he was faithful to his Egyptian master, he eventually ended up in prison, chained with fetters of iron.

How did Joseph respond to that situation? Did he say to himself, "Everything has gone wrong; the Lord's promise will never come true"? No, I do not believe he did. A process was going on in

Through the Psalms

Joseph; he was being tested. "Until the time that his word came to pass, the word of the Lord tested him."

When the Lord gives us a word of promise, there is a time fixed for its fulfillment. In the meantime, it often happens that events follow a course that seems exactly opposite to what God promised. In such a situation we must do as Joseph did. We must hold onto the promise, and not be tempted to think that God has failed or forgotten. The promise God gave us is testing us to see how we will conduct ourselves in the darkest hour. When we have passed the test and God's time has come, the promise will be fulfilled for us, just as it was for Joseph.

Faith's Response

I will accept God's testing as the prelude to the fulfillment of His promise.

The Miracle
of Redemption

He brought out Israel, laden with silver and
   gold,
      and from among their tribes no one faltered.

Psalm 105:37

The psalmist here describes the redemption of
Israel from Egypt under Moses. By the inspiration
of the Holy Spirit, he focuses on two aspects: the
financial and the physical. Financially, the people
were "laden with silver and gold." Physically,
"among their tribes no one faltered." Out of three
million people there was not one who was weak
or sickly, not one who could not face the long
desert march that lay ahead.

Just 24 hours previously, these same people had
been underprivileged slaves, ground down by centuries of poverty and oppression. What had brought
about this dramatic change? Just one thing: the
Passover lamb. As they applied its blood to their
doors and fed upon its flesh, they and their situation were totally transformed. Their poverty was

changed to wealth, their weakness to strength. A cowed rabble became an army, marching in well-ordered ranks.

Such is the fullness of God's redemption. It does not provide merely for our "souls." Its scope is also physical and financial. It covers every area of our personality and every need in our lives.

The redemption of Israel through the Passover lamb looked forward to a greater redemption that was to be provided through the Lamb of God, Jesus Christ. Paul reminds us, as Christians, that "Christ, our Passover lamb, has been sacrificed" (1 Corinthians 5:7). The sacrifice of Christ covers all that was accomplished through the Passover lamb in Egypt. More than that, it never has to be repeated, and its efficacy is eternal.

Faith's Response

Grant me faith, Lord Jesus, to receive all that You have provided for me through Your sacrifice.

Overshadowed

He spread out a cloud as a covering,
and a fire to give light at night.

Psalm 105:39

This describes how the Lord guided and protected His people Israel on their forty-year journey through the desert of Sinai. He spread out a cloud as a covering in the daytime and in the night gave them fire that provided both light and warmth. It so happens that as a soldier in World War II, I made a journey of seven days and nights through that same Sinai desert. I learned something there that greatly enhanced my appreciation of the wonders of God's provision. In the daytime the desert is very hot, but at night it becomes bitterly cold.

I understood how beautifully God had provided. In the daytime that cloud was a shield that protected them from the heat of the sun's rays. But at night it became a fire that gave them both light and needed warmth. That is how God guided His people for forty years through the desert.

For us as Christians, the cloud that guided Israel vividly prefigures the place of the Holy Spirit in our lives. Paul tells us that "those who are led by the Spirit of God are sons of God" (Romans 8:14). As God guided Israel through the desert by the cloud, He now guides us through this world by the Holy Spirit. What the cloud was to Israel, the Holy Spirit is to us. In times of heat, He overshadows us. In times of darkness, He gives us light. When it becomes cold all around us, He gives us supernatural warmth. In all circumstances our environment is tempered by His presence.

All this is summed up in the title by which Jesus promised the Spirit to His disciples: the Comforter.

Faith's Response

Help me, Lord, to be continually guided and overshadowed by Your Holy Spirit.

God in the Rock

He opened the rock, and water gushed out;
like a river it flowed in the desert.

Psalm 105:41

That is a picture of God's provision for His people
Israel in the forty years of their wandering in the
desert. It was a dry and barren land where there
were no rivers, no streams, no pools, and where
water was almost nonexistent. Yet God provided
water for them in abundance. He provided it in a
most unlikely way: out of a rock. When you look
at a rock in the desert, as I have done countless
times, it seems hard and unyielding. What good
could possibly come of it?

In the disguise of the rock, however, we understand that God Himself was with the people; "for
they drank from the spiritual rock that accompa-
nied them, and that rock was Christ" (1 Corinthians 10:4). God Himself was the rock and out of
Himself there came provision for His people in
abundance.

It was important, too, that Israel know how to approach the rock. At one time Moses was commanded to strike it. At another time he was commanded to speak to it. Each time he approached it in faith and obedience, out of that seemingly barren and unfriendly rock gushed an abundance of water, which flowed like a river in the desert.

It is often so in our lives. We find ourselves in a time of barrenness when provision seems lacking. Yet God is there. He is there in the form of a rock—something that seems hard and unyielding, something we might be tempted to turn away from. But when we recognize God in it and approach Him in faith and obedience, then the rock becomes the source of our provision.

Faith's Response

Teach me, Lord, to recognize You in the rock and to approach You aright.

Prayers We Should Not Pray

They soon forgat his works; they waited not for
   his counsel:
But lusted exceedingly in the wilderness, and
   tempted God in the desert.
And he gave them their request; but sent leanness into their soul.

Psalm 106:13–15 KJV

God had redeemed Israel out of Egypt. He had per-
formed stupendous miracles on their behalf. He had
made provision for them in all their desert wanderings. They had no need which He had not supplied. But Israel made two tragic errors. Their first
was forgetfulness: "They soon forgat his works."
Their second was impatience: "They waited not for
his counsel."

The food God provided for Israel was manna—
"the bread of heaven"—which fully supplied their
need of nourishment. The people, however, des-
pised this supernatural provision. Yielding to inor-
dinate appetite, they demanded meat instead. In

response, God caused a wind to carry quails into their camp, until they found themselves knee deep in quails. Then as the people began to feed on the quails, many were struck with sickness and died. Upon this the psalmist comments: "He gave them their request; but sent leanness into their soul."

We need to learn from Israel's fate and guard against these two related errors of forgetfulness and impatience. We, too, can be tempted to despise God's provision and feel that we know better than He does what we need. Then we begin to press our own self-willed desires upon God in prayer. In such a situation the worst thing God can do for us is grant our request. For if He does, it will produce "leanness in our soul."

Faith's Response

May I never press upon God a request that, if granted, would produce leanness in my soul.

At Death's Door

Fools, because of their rebellious way,
And because of their iniquities, were afflicted.
Their soul abhorred all kinds of food,
And they drew near to the gates of death.
Then they cried out to the LORD in their trouble;
He saved them out of their distresses.
He sent His word and healed them,
And delivered them from their destructions.

Psalm 107:17–20 NASB

"Fools, because of their rebellious way . . . were afflicted." That, of course, does not describe you or me! It must surely apply to people from some other group, or with some other problem. Or could it be that you and I, by our folly and rebelliousness, do sometimes bring sickness on ourselves? At any rate, the people here described have come to the end of the road. Their appetite gone, past all human help, they lie at death's door.

Finally, in utter desperation, they turn to God. They have certainly waited terribly long to pray, yet God in His mercy comes to their help. His mercy is threefold: He saves, He heals, He delivers. These are the three ways in which God meets humanity's basic needs: He saves from sin; He heals from sickness; He delivers from the power of Satan.

In each case God's answer comes through His Word. "He sent His word"—to save, to heal, to deliver. Here is a revelation of vital importance: Our problems may be different, but God's answer comes to each of us through the same channel—His Word.

Perhaps you have been crying out to God for help and you feel He has not answered you. Look against His Word. Ask the Holy Spirit to help you. You will find your answer there!

Faith's Response

Lord, I do believe You have the answer I need in Your Word. Help me to find it there.

God's Purpose
for My Tongue

O God, my heart is fixed; I will sing and give
praise, even with my glory.

Psalm 108:1 KJV

David has taken a firm decision: No matter what
happens, he is going to praise the Lord. This is the
only sufficient basis for praise that truly glorifies
God. If our praise arises merely out of our feelings
or our circumstances, it will be as uncertain and
fluctuating as they are. It must be based, as David's
was, on a firm decision of our will.

David's decision arose out of a special insight
contained in the closing phrase: "Even with my
glory." What does he have in mind when he says
"my glory"? This is one of those cases where the
Bible provides the best commentary on itself. In
Psalm 16:9 David uses the same phrase: "My glory
rejoiceth" (KJV). In Acts 2:26 Peter quotes this
verse, but changes one significant word: "My
tongue was glad" (KJV). Thus *glory* and *tongue* are
synonymous.

What a wonderful insight: My tongue is my "glory"! Consider the implications of that! Why did my Creator give me a tongue? That I might glorify Him with its praise. It is my supreme duty in life to glorify God, but out of all the members of my body there is one created specifically for this function: my tongue. Only when I glorify God with my tongue am I using it aright. Every other use is a misuse.

Let me, then, make the same decision as David: to use my tongue always and only for the purpose for which it was created.

Faith's Response

By a decision of my will I now determine to use my tongue for the purpose for which God gave it to me.

In the Day of Battle

Your troops will be willing
   on your day of battle.
Arrayed in holy majesty,
   from the womb of the dawn
   your young men will come to you like the
   dew.*

Psalm 110:3

*Alternative marginal translation

God is a God of battles. He is a Man of war. One of His main titles is *Lord of hosts*, that is, "Lord of armies." He appeared to Joshua as the captain of the Lord's army. Scripture reveals that the present age will close with a tremendous conflict between the forces of God and the forces of Satan. For this, God is now gathering His army.

David looks forward to this day and says, "Your troops will be willing on your day of battle"—more literally, "Your troops will be freewill offerings." God is not asking us at this time for offerings—our money or our talents or our time. He is asking for

Through the Psalms

one thing only: *ourselves.* We ourselves are to be His freewill offerings.

David paints vivid word pictures of this army. It comes "from the womb of the dawn"—brought forth by a birth out of darkness, as dawn follows night. "Arrayed in holy majesty," it shines "like the dew" illuminated by the rising sun. What is more pure or beautiful than a drop of dew as it is touched by the sun's first rays?

Such is the army God is now gathering. Out of the darkness of the past there is coming a new day—a day of birth and of battle. Young men in the dew of youth are being summoned, not to bring an offering, but to lay down their lives as God's freewill offerings in the day of battle.

Faith's Response

Accept me, Lord, as a freewill offering in Your day of battle.

Wisdom's Foundation

The fear of the LORD is the beginning of wisdom;
all who follow his precepts have good
understanding.

Psalm 111:10

The psalmist speaks of two wonderful qualities: wisdom and understanding. He points out that each of these has a moral foundation. The foundation for wisdom is the fear of the Lord. The foundation for understanding is following the Lord's precepts. Where these qualities are lacking, we should not expect either true wisdom or understanding.

We need to observe a distinction between wisdom and understanding on the one hand, and cleverness and intellectual education on the other. There are many clever, educated people who do not have wisdom or understanding. It could be argued, in fact, that most of the trouble in the world today is caused by educated fools. Cleverness is a matter of the mind, but wisdom springs from the heart. The intellect is an instrument whose use is determined by the heart.

A highly educated intellect may be compared to a very sharp knife. One man uses the knife to cut up food for his family; another may use it to kill his neighbor. It is irresponsible to place such a knife in the hands of a man who cannot be trusted to use it aright. Too long the devotees of secular humanism have worshiped at the shrine of the intellect. It is time for us to lay again the moral foundations of true wisdom and understanding.

Faith's Response

Help me, Lord, to meet the moral requirements for attaining to wisdom and understanding.

Sharing God's Loftiness

Who is like the Lord our God,
Who is enthroned on high,
Who humbles Himself to behold
The things that are in heaven and in the earth?
He raises the poor from the dust
And lifts the needy from the ash heap,
To make them sit with princes,
With the princes of His people.

Psalm 113:5–8 NASB

The psalmist portrays two aspects of God's nature that seem opposite, yet are beautifully combined in Him. On one side is God's lofty grandeur. He is enthroned on high. He humbles Himself merely to look down at things in heaven, much more those on earth. On the other side is God's tender compassion for the poor and the needy. He raises them from the dust—even from the ash heap—to set them with the princes of His people.

Through the prophet Isaiah God unfolds the same paradox, saying, "I live in a high and holy place, but also with him who is contrite and lowly in spirit . . ." (Isaiah 57:15). God does not exclude the lowly from His lofty dwelling. On the contrary, they are the ones whom He invites to share it with Him.

Traditionally, many of us have been given some understanding of God's awesome grandeur. This is a common theme of both preachers and poets. But only the Holy Spirit can reveal to us the other side of God's nature: His tender compassion and condescension.

Contrasting God's lofty majesty with our own position in the dust and the ash heap, we have felt ourselves totally unworthy of access to God, much less of fellowship with Him. We need to apprehend the divine paradox: It is our very lowliness that qualifies us to share God's loftiness.

Faith's Response

Out of my lowliness, Lord, I accept the invitation to share Your loftiness.

Choosing Life

I will not die but live,
and will proclaim what the Lord has done.

Psalm 118:17

Our attitude toward life needs to be totally positive. We cannot afford to be in any way negative or pessimistic or death-oriented. How many people yield to the pressure of some situation and exclaim, "I wish I were dead!" Little do they realize that this death wish opens the way for all sorts of dark, negative forces to come swarming into their minds, and eventually to take over their personalities. What began as an idle, thoughtless reaction to a passing pressure can end as tragic reality.

In Deuteronomy 30:19 Moses confronts the Israelites with this very issue: "This day . . . I have set before you life and death, blessings and curses. Now choose life, so that you and your children may live. . . ." How many of us realize that life requires a choice on our part? We are not free to submit to circumstances with passive indifference and say, "What comes will come." God sets a

Through the Psalm

choice before us: on the one hand, life and blessings; on the other hand, death and curses. We cannot evade the issue. Not to choose is to make the wrong choice.

The choice we make will affect not only ourselves, but also our descendants. Choosing life releases a stream that will flow down to succeeding generations.

Jesus said: "The thief comes only to steal and kill and destroy; I have come that they may have life, and have it to the full" (John 10:10). To whom shall we yield—to Jesus or to the thief?

Faith's Response

This day, Lord, according to Your Word, I choose life for myself and my descendants.

Building on God's Laws

I am a stranger on earth;
   do not hide your commands from me.
My soul is consumed with longing
   for your laws at all times.

Psalm 119:19–20

David has come face-to-face with himself in the mirror of reality, and he exclaims, "I am a stranger on earth." To almost every one of us there comes such a moment of truth when we, too, must acknowledge that this present world is not our home. People or things that we leaned on are suddenly taken away. Everything around us appears transitory and impermanent. Our life itself is a mist that hangs suspended in the air for a few moments and then passes, to return no more.

People react to this realization in different ways. Some turn to the pursuit of pleasure and entertainment, but find little of true satisfaction. Others bury themselves in work, never pausing to ask how much of permanent value all their work will accomplish. Still others deaden themselves with

alcohol or narcotics, or take refuge in a fantasy world of their own making.

David, however, turned to a different source: God's laws. He looked beneath the temporary and the transient. He realized that all life is ultimately governed by the laws of God. They are truly permanent and unchanging. By building his life upon them, he realized he could find a stability and security not subject to all the vicissitudes of the world around him.

The evidence of his success is provided by one simple historical fact: three thousand years later countless men and women still find abiding comfort in the psalms of David.

Faith's Response

Let me, too, build my life on the eternal, unchanging laws of God.

A Heart Set Free

> I run in the path of your commands,
> for you have set my heart free.

Psalm 119:32

What does it mean to be free? Does it mean that you do anything you please at any time? That you throw off all discipline and restraint, and indulge every whim and desire as it arises? That is the picture of freedom many people have today, but it does not correspond with the facts of human experience. We may crown self king over our lives, but we soon discover that self is only a puppet, directed by unseen powers over which it has no control. In reality, the indulgence of self is slavery to sin and to Satan.

David discovered a different kind of freedom—a freedom that comes only from God. He says, "You have set my heart free." What is the evidence of this freedom? "I run in the path of your commands." The freedom David discovered did not consist in indulging his own whims and desires. Rather, it was a freedom to obey God and do His will. An old prayer of the Church declares that God's service is perfect freedom. The Latin original goes further and says that to serve God is to reign as a king.

I meet some professing believers who are offering God a bare minimum. Their attitude seems to be: What is the least I can do and still be "saved"? Not so with David. There is exhilaration in the way he describes his freedom. He does not merely walk in the path of obedience to God. He actually runs. He finds himself obeying God not reluctantly or grudgingly, but freely and joyfully.

Such is the scriptural evidence of a heart truly set free.

Faith's Response

I renounce the deception of self-indulgence and commit myself wholly to the service of God.

Revived by God's Word

Remember the word to Your servant,
In which You have made me hope.
This is my comfort in my affliction,
That Your word has revived me.

Psalm 119:49–50 NASB

Has it occurred to you that there are times when we can remind God of something? David does that here. He reminds God of a promise God had given him. He says, in effect, "I am holding on to Your promise, Lord. It is my only source of hope. I am looking to You for its fulfillment."

Many times in the Bible, God shaped the lives of His servants by the specific, personal promises that He gave them. This was true of Abraham, Joseph, Moses and many others. In each case, the course of their lives was directed by the outworking of the promises God had made. In times of darkness, they went back to these promises and lifted them up afresh to God.

Does this mean God needs to be reminded by us, in case He should forget His own words? No, I

do not believe that. It may happen, however, that we receive a promise and hold it in our hearts—perhaps for many years—but it remains dormant, like seed beneath the soil. Then, at a moment of the Holy Spirit's prompting, we reaffirm to God our faith in what He has promised us. This produces two related results. It releases the power of God within the promise to bring about its fulfillment. At the same time, it imparts new life and strength to us. This is why David goes on to say, "Thy word has revived me."

For us also today, knowing how to respond to God's promises is the key to the fulfillment of His plan for our lives.

Faith's Response

I reaffirm my faith, Lord, in every promise You have given me.

Time to Consider

I have considered my ways
   and have turned my steps to your statutes.
I will hasten and not delay
   to obey your commands.

Psalm 119:59–60

From time to time in the midst of life we need to pause and consider our ways. It is easy to become so preoccupied with an endless succession of activities that we forget our overall objectives. We devote so much attention to the individual trees in our life that we lose sight of the forest that is God's eternal purpose. When this happens, we need to stop and ask ourselves two basic questions: First, what is the end purpose of all that I am doing? Second, am I achieving that purpose?

The failure to face these basic issues can lead to a sense of frustration that defies analysis. We are doing a lot of seemingly important things, yet are inwardly dissatisfied and not seeing the results we expect. This was exactly the problem with which Haggai confronted the Jewish people in his day:

"Give careful thought to your ways. You have planted much, but have harvested little. You eat, but never have enough. You drink, but never have your fill. You put on clothes, but are not warm. You earn wages, only to put them in a purse with holes in it" (Haggai 1:5–6).

David, too, had experienced this kind of frustration in his life, and he shows us the remedy he had discovered: to bring our lives into line with God's statutes; to make obedience to His commands our first priority. This will restore harmony and productivity to all the other areas of our life.

Faith's Response

Beginning today, I will bring my life into line with God's statutes and commandments.

Friendship
with God's People

I am a friend to all who fear you,
to all who follow your precepts.

Psalm 119:63

When you tell someone you are a Christian, you
may usually anticipate a certain kind of response:
What denomination do you belong to? What church
do you attend? Are you a Baptist, a Methodist, a
Lutheran, a Catholic? For my part, I question
whether God is as much concerned about these
labels as some human beings are. I, at least, am not
interested in being pigeonholed according to a de-
nominational label. Once people have put me into
one of their little religious "boxes," their minds are
no longer open to the issues that really matter. I pre-
fer them to relate to me as a person, not as a religious exhibit.

When people ask me, therefore, what denomination I belong to, I like to answer in the words
of David: "I am a friend to all who fear God and
follow His precepts." This places the emphasis on

the primary issues: my relationship with God and with His people.

My first wife, Lydia, once shocked a Catholic lady, who was our neighbor, by remarking casually, "Of course there won't be any Catholics in heaven." As the lady stood open-mouthed with shock and astonishment, Lydia quickly added, "There won't be any Protestants either. Heaven is for those who love and obey God."

We do not have to wait until we reach heaven to make this discovery. Already here on earth, between people such as David describes, there is a bond of love and inner understanding that transcends all human religious labels.

Faith's Response

Give me a heart of love, Lord, for all who fear you and follow Your precepts.

Learning from Affliction

Before I was afflicted I went astray,
   but now I obey your word. . . .
It was good for me to be afflicted
   so that I might learn your decrees.
I know, O Lord, that your laws are righteous,
   and in faithfulness you have afflicted me.

Psalm 119:67, 71, 75

If ever a man had to face affliction, it was David. Yet he did not become bitter or discouraged. In fact, looking back on it, he was grateful for it. He realized it had done him good. In his words here quoted, David shares with us two vitally important lessons he learned from his affliction.

The first lesson relates to God's motive in permitting us to come under affliction. God does not do it because He is angry with us or has rejected us. On the contrary, it is the expression of His faithfulness. He sees us taking a wrong course that will lead us to our own harm and ultimate ruin, so he sends affliction to turn us back into the way that leads to peace and blessing.

The second lesson concerns our response to affliction. David did not view affliction as a disaster. Rather, he saw it as a kind of corrective medicine. It was something he needed to adjust his life. "Before I was afflicted, I went astray," he says, "but I suffered for it. Now I've learned my lesson: It pays to obey Your word."

Are you in the midst of affliction? Do not fight back and do not argue with God. Acknowledge that God is afflicting you in His faithfulness. He has a reason. Ask Him what it is. He is seeking to turn you back from something harmful and to bring you into something beneficial. If you are willing to learn from your present affliction, there will come a time when you will look back with gratitude on the benefits you have received.

Faith's Response

I acknowledge that You have a reason for afflicting me, Lord. Help me to learn my lesson.

Settled in Heaven

Forever, O LORD,
Your word is settled in heaven.

Psalm 119:89 NASB

Over many centuries man has sought through speculation and reasoning to discover the nature of God, but he has always ended in frustration. Different philosophers, all claiming to apply pure reason, have arrived at completely different conclusions: God is perfect mind; God is total reality; God is immanent in all existence; there is no God; and so on.

Over against all such speculations, God has sovereignly chosen to reveal Himself, not to man's reason, but to his faith. The primary channel of God's self-revelation is the unique Book He has caused to be written, the Bible. In the words of David here quoted, the Bible tells us three wonderful facts about itself.

The first fact is contained in the opening word: *forever.* The Bible is eternal. It is not affected by the passage of time. It does not change with fashions,

or the events of history, or the attitudes or thoughts of man. It endures forever.

Second, David speaks of *Your word*. It is God's Word, not man's. It originates with God, not man. It is the revelation of God Himself—His ways, His thoughts, His attitudes, His purposes, His laws. Men were the channel through which it came, but always God was the source.

Third, this word is *settled in heaven*. Nothing that happens on earth can ever unsettle it. It is not subject to the decrees of kings or emperors, or to the opinions of politicians, or to the violence of armies. It is out of reach of all evil forces. Ultimately it determines the course of all events on earth.

Faith's Response

I receive by faith God's revelation of Himself to me and bow to its authority in my life.

The Purpose
of God's Laws

Your faithfulness continues through all
    generations;
    you established the earth, and it endures.
Your laws endure to this day,
    for all things serve you.

Psalm 119:90–91

The force that controls the universe is not purely
physical. It cannot be expressed fully in the concepts of mathematical physics. These are true to a
point, but they do not contain the whole truth.
The so-called "laws" of the universe do not result
merely from the random interplay of inanimate
forces. The ultimate reality behind the universe is
a Person: God. The very word *law* is meaningless
without a lawgiver—one who enacts and enforces
the law. The laws that man discerns in the universe are the visible expression of the faithfulness
of the invisible Creator.

Not only do these laws originate from God; they
also serve God. God did not simply set the uni-

verse in motion, and then retire to the position of a detached spectator. He has eternal purposes that continue to be worked out in the ongoing course of the universe. What a wonderful revelation! Everything in the universe is continually obeying God's laws and serving His purposes.

Writing to the church at Corinth, Paul takes this revelation one step further: "For all things are for your sakes" (2 Corinthians 4:15 NASB). Not merely does the whole universe obey the laws of God; not merely do these laws all serve God's purposes; but—most wonderful of all—the purposes thus being worked out center in God's people. They are all designed and operated to bring about the highest possible good for those who are the objects of God's redeeming love and care.

Faith's Response

I acknowledge God's laws at work throughout the universe and I believe their purpose is my highest good.

Anchored to God's Law

> If your law had not been my delight,
>   I would have perished in my affliction.
> I will never forget your precepts,
>   for by them you have preserved my life.

Psalm 119:92–93

Affliction is part of the total pattern of life in this world. It is unrealistic, therefore, to expect to avoid it. Some Christians imagine that their faith will grant them automatic exemption from affliction, but this is not so. If anything, the opposite is to be expected. Paul and Barnabas told a newly formed Christian congregation, "We must go through many hardships to enter the kingdom of God" (Acts 14:22). Do not look for a way through life that bypasses affliction. If by any chance you should find one, it would not lead you into God's Kingdom.

David certainly did not escape the stormy waves and blasts of affliction, but he did have an anchor that held him firm in the midst of them. That anchor was God's law. David's heart was so bound by love to God's law that affliction could not move him. Looking back on all he had passed through, he says with gratitude to the Lord: "I will never forget your precepts, for by them you have preserved my life."

The same anchor is still available to us today: the eternal, unchanging law of God. The tempests of affliction cannot shift its foundations or diminish its authority. We make it our anchor as David made it his—by the unreserved commitment of our obedience. Out of this there flows a stream of life within stronger than all the forces that oppose us from without.

Faith's Response

Lord, I yield my heart in unreserved obedience to Your eternal law.

The Next Step

Your word is a lamp to my feet
and a light for my path.

Psalm 119:105

David is here concerned about the way we are to walk through this world. He focuses on the two main elements in our walk: the feet that we walk with and the path that we walk on. He offers us the blessed assurance that if we fully trust and obey God's Word, we never need to walk in darkness.

There will be times when the world around us will be in total darkness. We will not be able to see more than a few feet in any direction. There may be unsolved problems ahead. There may be dangers around the corner. But in the midst of it all we have this guarantee: If we are sincerely obeying the Word of God as it is revealed to us in any given situation, we will never walk in the dark. We will never put our foot in some treacherous place that will cause us to stumble and fall into injury or disaster.

Through the Psalms

This guarantee, however, applies only to one specific area: the place where we are to plant our next footstep. God does not promise us that we will be able to see more than one step ahead. Beyond that, we may have no way of knowing what awaits us—but that is not our concern. All that God requires of us is to take the next step of simple obedience to His Word.

Our greatest danger is that we will seek to peer too far ahead into the darkness. In so doing we may miss the place for our next step, which is the only area illuminated for us at that moment.

Faith's Response

Lord, show me where to plant my foot just now in obedience to Your Word, and I will leave the future in Your hands.

Embracing
God's Commands

Because I love your commands
   more than gold, more than pure gold,
and because I consider all your precepts right,
   I hate every wrong path.

Psalm 119:127–128

What is your attitude toward God's commands?
Do you fear them? Resent them? Try to get away
from them? That is a foolish attitude. God gave us
His commands not to create problems for us, but
to solve them; not to harm us, but to help us. God's
love is in His commands. They are given to save
us from ourselves, to save us from evil, to show us
the way out of our difficulties and problems.

David had learned that. That is why he said to
God, "I love your commands more than gold, more
than pure gold." What is more precious than gold?
Nothing in this created world. But God's commands are infinitely more precious. David understood that. Instead of running from God's commands, therefore, or resenting them, or obeying

Through the Psalms

them reluctantly, he embraced them as the tokens of God's love for him.

Love of God's commands automatically produced in David a corresponding attitude of hatred toward every wrong path—everything contrary to those commands. There can be no neutrality in moral issues. Love and obedience to God's commands will cause us to recognize and turn away from all the deceptive disguises under which evil masquerades. Walking in the light of those commands keeps us from everything harmful and destructive.

Faith's Response

I embrace God's commands as the tokens of His love for me and I renounce all compromise with evil.

Promises That Stand the Test

Your promises have been thoroughly tested,
and your servant loves them.

Psalm 119:140

What comfort and assurance David offers us out of his own experience! *God's promises have been thoroughly tested.* They are not mere theories, not just abstract theology. In all the different circumstances of life, they stand the test.

To this testimony of David my own heart echoes *Amen!* For more than sixty years I have lived by the promises of God. I have proved them in many different circumstances: in war, in famine, in sickness, in loneliness, in bereavement, in misunderstanding. When I had lain for one year in the hospital with a condition the doctors were not able to cure, I turned to God's promises and received a complete and lasting healing. When my first wife was called home after we had spent thirty years together, God's promises of comfort met my need as no human comfort could do. Like David therefore, I want to recommend God's promises to you. There is a promise to meet every need that arises in our life—and every one of them stands the test.

Perhaps you have been disillusioned, hurt, disappointed, because some person—or persons—have made promises to you and then failed to keep them. God is not like that. He keeps all His promises. Do not be discouraged if people have let you down. Do not become embittered or cynical, because that will only harm you. Just turn your eyes to God. Focus on His faithfulness. Put your trust in His promises. They have been thoroughly tested.

Faith's Response

Show me, Lord, how to appropriate the promises of Your Word that will meet each need in my life.

The Key to Peace

Great peace have they who love your law,
and nothing can make them stumble.

Psalm 119:165

The Bible promises not just peace, but *great peace*.
Unfortunately, our contemporary speech has been
so debased that it is hard for us to appreciate the
full scope of what God is offering us. In the world
today we have a very low view of peace. If two
nations are not actually fighting one another with
weapons of war, we call that peace. There may be
hatred, fear, verbal abuse and recrimination, but
we still speak about peace.

The Bible has a much higher standard. The
Hebrew word for peace is *shalom*. It means more
than just the absence of strife or war. It is con-
nected with a root that means completeness or
wholeness. So peace is wholeness, completeness.
It implies that there is nothing lacking in our life.
A person who has peace in this sense is a complete
person and leads a full life.

This is the kind of life promised to those who love the law of God, for His law is as wide in its scope as peace. It covers every area of our lives—spiritual, emotional, physical, material. As we bring each of these areas under the law of God, we find ourselves in harmony with the universe around us, for that, too, is governed by the same law. Then nothing can make us stumble. We are not easily offended or discouraged. Opposition and difficulties do not overthrow us, because the out-working of God's law within us is stronger than anything that can come against us from without.

Faith's Response

Bring my whole life under Your law, Lord, and release Your peace within me.

Never-Failing Help

I will lift up my eyes to the mountains;
From where shall my help come?
My help comes from the LORD,
Who made heaven and earth.
He will not allow your foot to slip;
He who keeps you will not slumber.

Psalm 121:1–3 NASB

The psalmist looks at the mountains in their majesty and grandeur, and then he asks a question, "From whence shall my help come?" He is not expecting his help to come from the mountains. They serve, however, to remind him of the One who created the mountains and the seas and the whole earth. He realizes that this Creator is also his Helper. The magnitude and grandeur of the visible creation provide him with a standard by which to measure the divine resources that are personally available to him.

At times we, too, need to contemplate the might and the marvels of creation and to apply the psalmist's lesson to ourselves. This Creator is also

our Keeper. Day and night He watches over us and upholds us. He never falls asleep.

I once watched a little boy being carried on his father's arm, and I noticed how tightly he clutched his father's lapel. After a while, however, he fell asleep and his hand slipped away from the lapel. Yet his father continued to hold him just as securely. The boy's security did not depend on his holding onto his father, but only on his father keeping hold of him.

So it is in our relationship with God. Sometimes we feel that if we do not hold on tightly enough to God, we will fall. But the fact is that God continues to hold us, even if we let go of Him. We may fall asleep, but He never does.

Faith's Response

Whether I am weak or strong, awake or asleep, I thank You, Lord, that You uphold me just the same.

Complete Protection

> The LORD will protect you from all evil;
> He will keep your soul.
> The LORD will guard your going out and your
>   coming in
> From this time forth and forever.
>
> Psalm 121:7–8 NASB

In the version here quoted, three different but closely related words are used to describe the Lord's watchcare: He will *protect, keep, guard.* In the original Hebrew, the same word is used all through. Yet these variations in translation serve to bring out the manyfaceted completeness of God's care for us. It covers every danger, every situation, every form of attack.

The Lord will protect our soul from all *evil.* This is not a guarantee that we will be spared trials, or hardships, or sorrows. It is, rather, an assurance that none of these will ever be able to bring us under the dominion of sin or Satan. In the midst of them all, our soul will be preserved inviolate.

The Lord will protect our *going out* and our *coming in.* He will be with us not only when we begin

Through the Psalm

each journey, but when we come to the end; not only when we go out fresh to work in the morning, but also when we return home tired in the evening.

The Lord's protection is *from this time forth and forever*. It extends throughout time and on into eternity. He protects us on each journey that we take through time. Then, when the moment comes for us to step out of time and into eternity, His presence will still be with us. He will see us safely through the narrow gates of death and out into the fullness of eternity. When we complete that last journey, He will be there to welcome us home—*forever*.

Faith's Response

My almighty Creator, I commit to You every journey I will ever take from now on and forever.

Closely Compacted Together

Jerusalem is built like a city
    that is closely compacted together.

Psalm 122:3

That phrase *closely compacted together* gives us a revelation of how God's people are to be united. In
the Hebrew language, almost every word is formed
from a root of three consonants. If you want to
know the real meaning of the word, therefore, you
have to trace it back to its root. The word translated *closely compacted together* is formed from a root
which means a "friend," a "comrade," someone
very close to you. It has no special "religious" asso-
ciations. Rather, it denotes a basic human relationship, warm and uncomplicated. It still has the
same meaning today in modern Hebrew.

Over the centuries the Church has substituted
various other religious requirements as the basis
for unity: attending a special place of worship;
meeting together a certain number of times each
week; subscribing to certain statements of doc-

trine. History has demonstrated, however, that none of these provides a solid or sufficient basis for unity. The psalmist's description of Jerusalem still offers the only real key. The strength of the Church rests on personal relationships, not on meetings or doctrines.

What makes God's people truly one is personal commitment: first and foremost, to the Lord Himself; second, to all who are likewise committed to Him. This mortar of personal commitment holds us together even when we disagree on doctrine, or do not meet at the same time or place. It makes us friends and comrades, *closely compacted together.*

Faith's Response

Give me grace, Lord, to make an unreserved commitment to You and to my fellow believers.

Peace Through Prayer

Pray for the peace of Jerusalem:
they shall prosper that love thee.

Psalm 122:6 KJV

This call to prayer for Jerusalem is addressed to all who accept the Bible as God's authoritative Word. God requires all His people from every nation and every background to be concerned about the peace of one particular city: *Jerusalem.*

For this there is an important, practical reason. God's purpose for this age will climax in the setting up of His Kingdom. Each time we pray the familiar words *Thy Kingdom come,* we are aligning ourselves with this purpose. We must remember, however, that the prayer continues, *Thy will be done in earth, as it is in heaven.* It is *on earth* that God's Kingdom is to be established. His Kingdom is invisible as yet to human eyes, but it is not something vague or amorphous. Ultimately it will have a tangible, earthly realization.

The capital and center of God's Kingdom on earth will be the city of Jerusalem. The adminis-

tration of righteous government will go forth from Jerusalem to all nations on earth. In response, the gifts and worship of these nations will flow back to Jerusalem. Thus the peace and prosperity of all nations depend upon that of Jerusalem. Until Jerusalem enters into her peace, no nation on earth can know true or lasting peace.

To all who heed God's call to love Jerusalem and pray for her peace, God gives a special, precious promise: They shall prosper. The word translated *prosper* goes beyond the material realm. It denotes a deep inner well-being, a freedom from care and anxiety. As we align ourselves with God's plan for world peace by praying for Jerusalem, we experience even now a foretaste of that peace.

Faith's Response

Lord, I do now align myself with Your plan and I commit myself to pray for the peace of Jerusalem.

Stability, Security, Rest

Those who trust in the Lord are like Mount
   Zion,
   which cannot be shaken but endures forever.
As the mountains surround Jerusalem,
   so the Lord surrounds his people
   both now and forevermore.

Psalm 125:1–2

For the Lord has chosen Zion,
   he has desired it for his dwelling:
"This is my resting place for ever and ever. . . ."

Psalm 132:13–14

In these beautiful word pictures, the psalmist
describes three of the most blessed provisions of
God for His people: stability, security and rest. The
world craves these blessings and seeks them in
various ways, but never finds them in true or abiding form. Yet there is a place where we may find
all three. It is pictured as a mountain, Zion, and as
a city, Jerusalem.

Mount Zion pictures *stability.* All other mountains
will be shaken, all other hills removed (Isaiah

54:10). But Mount Zion cannot be shaken. It is unique among all earth's mountains, because God has set it apart for His own dwelling place.

Jerusalem pictures *security*. All who have ever traveled to Jerusalem can confirm the accuracy of the psalmist's description. No matter from what point of the compass you approach the city, you must pass through mountains to reach it, for they surround it on all sides. In like manner, the presence of almighty God surrounds His people.

Stability and security, in turn, offer us *rest*, never-ending rest. God has declared: "This is my resting place for ever and ever. . . ." Sharing God's dwelling, and surrounded by His presence, we enter into His rest.

Faith's Response

Founded on God's mountain, dwelling in God's city, I share His eternal rest.

The Watershed of History

"Many times they have persecuted me from my
    youth up,"
Let Israel now say,
"Many times they have persecuted me from my
    youth up;
Yet they have not prevailed against me. . . ."
May all who hate Zion
Be put to shame and turned backward;
Let them be like grass upon the housetops,
Which withers before it grows up. . . .

Psalm 129:1–2, 5–6 NASB

When God comes onto the stage of human history,
He does not descend from His throne in power and
majesty and demand instant obedience. Such obedience would be motivated by fear, and would not
necessarily indicate true submission from the heart.
Historically, therefore, God has come among men
in a variety of disguises. Those whose hearts were
humble and sincere penetrated the disguise and
responded appropriately. But the rebellious continued in their rebellion, not even aware that it was
almighty God whom they had rejected.

For more than three thousand years, from the time of the Exodus onward, God has chosen to identify Himself with Israel as His people. Amazingly, this has never been affected by Israel's weakness or waywardness. Even at a time when they were enduring divine judgment on their disobedience, the prophet Zechariah pronounced God's wrath against all the nations who had plundered them, but said to Israel: "He who touches you, touches the apple of His eye" (Zechariah 2:8 NASB).

Here the psalmist warns that those who fight against God's purpose for Israel will be like "grass upon the housetops." They may begin to sprout with unnatural rapidity, but their root has no soil. They will wither as quickly as they grew, and be left as a relic of history. The key to true prosperity, for individuals and for nations alike, is to discern God in His people and to identify with His purpose for them.

Today God is restoring Zion. Here is the watershed of history. Those who align themselves with the restoration of Zion will enjoy God's favor and blessing; those who oppose will wither like grass on the housetops.

Faith's Response

Lord, help me to discern You in Your people and to align myself with Your purpose for them.

Weaned from Arrogance

> My heart is not proud, O LORD,
>   my eyes are not haughty;
> I do not concern myself with great matters
>   or things too wonderful for me.
> But I have stilled and quieted my soul;
>   like a weaned child with its mother,
>   like a weaned child is my soul within me.
>
> Psalm 131:1–2

David describes a spiritual change that has taken place within him: He has become like a child weaned from its mother. What does he mean by that?

I have ministered in countries where women habitually nursed their babies in my meetings. Each time an infant would begin to cry and disturb the service, the mother would immediately pacify it by giving it the breast. Thus I came to appreciate in a practical way the difference between a weaned and an unweaned child. An unweaned child cries and expects something immediately from its mother. A weaned child leaves the initiative to its mother; it trusts her to serve food at the right time.

As a result of being "weaned," David no longer concerned himself with great matters or things too wonderful for him. We, too, must allow God to wean us from our natural, undisciplined arrogance that cries for answers to problems that are not our concern. Instead, we must learn to accept the spiritual food that God prepares for us at the time He sees fit to serve it.

Being weaned is a necessary stage in a child's progress to maturity. In my own life, since I have learned to leave the initiative with God, I find that I receive much more from Him. The diet of a weaned child is much more varied than that of an unweaned one.

Faith's Response

I renounce arrogance, Lord, and I trust You to give me my daily bread—both natural and spiritual.

The Place of Blessing

Behold, how good and how pleasant it is
For brothers to dwell together in unity!
It is like the precious oil upon the head,
Coming down upon the beard,
Even Aaron's beard,
Coming down upon the edge of his robes.
It is like the dew of Hermon,
Coming down upon the mountains of Zion;
For there the LORD commanded the blessing—
    life forever.

Psalm 133 NASB

What a powerful climax: *There the Lord commanded the blessing!* Of one thing I am confident: If the Lord commands the blessing, there is no power in the universe that can withhold it. Many times I see God's people crying out for His blessing and seeking it earnestly. I can sympathize with that; and yet is it not better to dwell in the place where God has commanded the blessing?

Where is that place? It is where brothers dwell together in unity. To "dwell together" is much more than merely coming together for an hour or

two on Sunday morning. It means sharing life together—the failures as well as the successes, the problems as well as the victories, the material as well as the spiritual.

David establishes a chain of consecutive truths: life flows out of blessing; blessing flows out of unity; and unity, like the anointing oil, flows from the head downward. Nothing flows more easily and smoothly than oil. But it only flows *downward,* never upward. David also compares unity to dew. This, too, always comes *down.*

So it is with the Body of Christ: Unity must begin with the leaders. Sheep cannot be united while their shepherds are divided. But once leaders can achieve true unity, it flows down over the rest of the Body. There God has already commanded the blessing. It is vain to run after it or strive for it, if we fail to meet the conditions.

Faith's Response

Lord, help me to find the place in Your Body where You have commanded the blessing.

God Has Made Himself Available

I will bow down toward your holy temple
and will praise your name
for your love and your faithfulness,
for you have exalted above all things
your name and your word.

Psalm 138:2

Here is a marvelous example of God's considera-
tion and compassion for us. He is a great God, a
mighty God, the Creator. We can see His wisdom
and His power manifested in countless different
aspects of creation. The heavens declare His glory;
the oceans manifest His power; the mountains
reveal His strength; the snowflakes illustrate His
wisdom. All these marvels of creation demonstrate
to us God's greatness. But there is one thing they
cannot do: They cannot make God available to us.

Outside of the realm of nature, however, there
are two other ways that God reveals Himself: His
name and His Word. These He has exalted above
all the demonstrations of His greatness provided

by creation. It is for our sakes He has done this, because through His name and His Word He does for us what creation cannot do: He makes Himself available to us.

God's Word opens to us those intimate aspects of His personality that nature cannot reveal. It tells us how we may receive His mercy and favor. It unfolds all that He has promised to do for us. God's name, in turn, makes all those promises available to us.

We cannot come to God on the basis of creation's marvels, but we can come to Him on the basis of the promises of His Word—and all these are made available to us in the name of His Son, Jesus Christ.

"I tell you the truth, my Father will give you whatever you ask in my name" (John 16:23).

Faith's Response

Thank You, Lord, for making Yourself available to me through Your Word and Your name.

His Purpose for Me

> The Lord will fulfill his purpose for me;
>   your love, O Lord, endures forever—
>   do not abandon the works of your hands.

Psalm 138:8

How good to know that God has a purpose for each one of us! David does not say that the Lord will fulfill *my* purpose; he says that the Lord will fulfill *His purpose for me.* There is a great difference—I may have one purpose, God may have another. God does not guarantee that He will fulfill my purpose, only that He will fulfill His purpose.

God's guarantee is contained in the words that follow: "Your love, O Lord, endures forever." The Hebrew word translated *love* means, more fully, the faithfulness that causes God to keep the commitments of the covenant He has made with us. God's commitment to fulfill His purpose in our lives extends through time and on into eternity.

David ends this verse with what sounds like a cry of desperation: "Do not abandon the works of your hands." I remember once ministering at the bedside of a committed Christian lady who was dying of cancer. Picking up a copy of The Living Bible from her night stand, she read aloud those words of David in that version: "You made me—don't abandon me!" This was her personal affirmation that neither sickness nor pain nor death itself could prevent God's covenant-keeping faithfulness from working out His purpose for her to its victorious conclusion.

For each of us who has entered into the covenant that God offers us through Jesus, the same assurance holds good. God made us; He will not abandon us. It may not be our purpose, but it will be His purpose. That purpose will stand sure and unshakable, no matter what we go through.

Faith's Response

I embrace God's purpose for me, even if it is different from my own, and I trust Him to fulfill it.

Respect for God's Temple

For you created my inmost being;
    you knit me together in my mother's womb.
I praise you because I am fearfully and wonder-
    fully made . . .
My frame was not hidden from you
    when I was made in the secret place.
When I was woven together in the depths of
        the earth,
    your eyes saw my unformed body.

                                    Psalm 139:13–16

Some years ago God spoke to me through this passage about the marvel of the physical body—my
own body, in particular. The body is a divine mas-
terpiece, planned ages in advance, made of materials
formed in the secret depths of the earth and knit
together in the womb by the Creator's invisible
hand. I became concerned that I treat this master-
piece of my body with the care and honor due to
it; that I maintain it in the best possible condition
to fulfill its God-appointed function.

Again and again throughout history, men have
sought to construct a building to accommodate

God. They have lavished time, labor and wealth upon it. At best, however, such a building can serve as a place to offer worship, never as God's dwelling. "The Most High does not live in houses made by men" (Acts 7:48).

God has a different plan. At the beginning of human history He fashioned a temple for Himself with His own hands: the body of man. Then He worked out the plan of redemption by which that body, sanctified by faith in Christ's sacrifice, could be offered back to Him to be a temple of His Holy Spirit.

"Do you not know that your body is a temple of the Holy Spirit, who is in you, whom you have received from God? You are not your own; you were bought at a price. Therefore honor God with your body" (1 Corinthians 6:19–20).

Faith's Response

Help me, Lord, to maintain the temple of my body in a condition that honors You.

The Fifth Column

Do I not hate those who hate you, O Lᴏʀᴅ,
  and abhor those who rise up against you?
I have nothing but hatred for them;
  I count them my enemies.

Psalm 139:21–22

Is it right for you and me, as Christians, to echo these words of David? Yes—if we also echo what David said in the next two verses: "Search me, O God, and know my heart. . . . See if there is any offensive way in me. . . ." The enemies of God we need to be most concerned about are not those who attack us from without, but those within our own hearts.

In 1936 there was a civil war in Spain that gave rise to the phrase *fifth column*. It happened that a Spanish general was beseiging a Spanish city, and a second general asked him about his plan to capture it. "I have four columns attacking the city," the first general replied, "from the north, the south, the east and the west. But it's my fifth column that I'm expecting to take the city for me."

"Where is your fifth column?" the second general asked. The reply was brief: "Inside the city."

So it is with us Christians. We can never be defeated from without, but if there is a fifth column of God's enemies in our hearts, that spells defeat.

A young man once confessed to me that he had a problem with lust. "But I rather enjoy it," he added. "Do you think God will deliver me?"

"Definitely not!" I replied. "God delivers us from our enemies, not from our friends."

We cannot afford to be friends with God's enemies.

Faith's Response

Show me, Lord, if I am harboring a "fifth column" in my heart, and help me to get rid of it.

Four Keys to Answered Prayer

> For the sake of Your name, O Lord, revive me.
> In Your righteousness bring my soul out of
>   trouble.
> And in Your lovingkindness, cut off my enemies
> And destroy all those who afflict my soul,
> For I am Your servant.
>
> Psalm 143:11–12 NASB

David was in deep trouble but, as so often, trouble became the source of inspiration to him. The prayer that resulted is a pattern we all need to study. In it, David provides us with four firm, unvarying reasons for believing God will answer our prayers.

First, *for the sake of Your name.* God's name gives us access to Him. Jesus promised His disciples, "My Father will give you whatever you ask in my name" (John 16:23).

Second, *in Your righteousness.* We dare not approach God in our own righteousness, but only in the righteousness of Jesus imputed to us on the basis of our faith. We come before God arrayed in a robe of His righteousness (Isaiah 61:10).

Third, *in Your lovingkindness*. The Hebrew word thus translated denotes the faithfulness of God in keeping His covenant commitments to His people. Our failures and weaknesses in no way change God's commitments to us.

Fourth, *I am Your servant*. This is an affirmation of our personal commitment to God, which He will invariably honor. He never abandons those who have given their lives to Him for His service.

There is one key word that occurs in all these four reasons: it is *Your*. The secret of successful prayer is to turn away from ourselves and to focus totally on the Person to whom we are praying.

Faith's response

May my troubles teach me to find God in prayer, just as David's taught him.

Religion That God Accepts

The LORD watches over the alien
and sustains the fatherless and the widow,
but he frustrates the ways of the wicked.

Psalm 146:9

The psalmist sets side-by-side two aspects of God's character that balance one another: on the one hand, His care for the stranger, the fatherless and the widow; and on the other hand, the severity of His dealings with the wicked. As Christians, we are not normally required to be instruments of God's judgment on the wicked, but we are required to express His compassion toward the needy—particularly the widow and the orphan.

We are prone to talk about religion in general terms, without realizing that the Bible offers us a very specific definition of what God accepts as genuine religion. Often God's use of the term is quite different from ours. Much that we regard as religious God does not accept as such.

Through the Psalms

God's definition is found in James 1:27: "Religion that God our Father accepts as pure and faultless is this: to look after orphans and widows in their distress and to keep oneself from being polluted by the world." There are two parts to this definition: on the positive side, practical care for widows and orphans; on the negative side, keeping ourselves from the world's pollutions. It is characteristic of "religious" people—as we think of them—that they are very strong in their stand against "worldliness," but that they often do little or nothing to help widows and orphans.

In today's world one thing is sure: If we are truly concerned to care for widows and orphans, there is no lack of opportunity. In country after country, their needs cry out to us. If we fail to respond, it is through lack of will, not opportunity.

Faith's Reponse

I accept my God-given responsibility toward the needy, especially widows and orphans.

He Calls the Stars
by Name

> He determines the number of the stars
>   and calls them each by name.
> Great is our Lord and mighty in power;
>   his understanding has no limit.

> Psalm 147:4–5

The psalmist gives us an objective, scientific standard by which to measure the knowledge and power of the Lord. Human astronomers would not dare to calculate the number of stars in the universe. They do tell us, however, that it amounts to billions upon billions. Yet God knows the exact number of the stars. He is in direct contact with each one and He controls its movements.

So totally accurate and reliable are the movements of the stars, that astronomers can compute mathematically where each star was thousands of years ago or where it will be thousands of years from now. But let us never attribute this precision to some mindless, impersonal force or "law." Behind it all is the infinite wisdom of a Creator whose concern extends to the remotest corner of His universe.

Furthermore, the psalmist tells us *how* God controls the stars: *He calls them each by name.* In the Bible, a name expresses the essential individual character of the person or object named. To God, even the stars are not mere mindless confirmations of matter to be identified only by location or magnitude. Each has its own name. Each responds to that name when God calls it.

If God deals thus with the stars, how much more with His own sons and daughters! Do you ever feel "lost" in the magnitude of the universe? Do you wonder whether you really matter? Then listen to your Creator, who is also your Redeemer: "Fear not, for I have redeemed you; I have summoned you by name; you are mine" (Isaiah 43:1).

Faith's Response

Open my ears to hear Your voice, Lord, each time You call me by name.

Topical Index

1. God's Eternal Majesty

4. Times of Pressure

5. God's All-Embracing Care

6. The Word at Work

7. Time and Eternity

Scripture Index

221

Derek Prince was born in India of British parents. He was educated as a scholar of Greek and Latin at Eton College and Cambridge University, England, where he held a Fellowship in Ancient and Modern Philosophy at King's College. He also studied Hebrew and Aramaic, both at Cambridge University and the Hebrew University in Jerusalem. In addition, he speaks a number of other modern languages.

While serving with the British army in World War II, he began to study the Bible and experienced a life-changing encounter with Jesus Christ. Out of this encounter he formed two conclusions: first, that Jesus Christ is alive; second, that the Bible is a true, relevant, up-to-date book. These conclusions altered the whole course of his life. Since then, he has devoted his life to studying and teaching the Bible.

His daily radio broadcast, *Today with Derek Prince,* reaches more than half the world and includes translations into Arabic, Chinese, Croatian, Malagasy, Mongolian, Russian, Samoan, Spanish and

Tongan. He is the author of over 40 books, over 450 audio and 150 video teaching cassettes, many of which have been translated and published in more than 60 languages.

Derek's main gift is explaining the Bible and its teaching in a clear and simple way. His nondenominational, nonsectarian approach has made his teaching equally relevant and helpful to people from all racial and religious backgrounds.

Also by Derek Prince

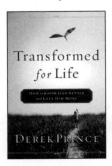

Transformed for Life
*How to
Know God Better
and Love Him More*
0-8007-9307-2

A compilation of six life-changing
books that all involve overcoming
trials and hardships and living life
transformed by the power of
Jesus Christ.

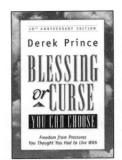

**Blessing or Curse: You
Can Choose, 2d ed.**
*Freedom from Pressures
You Thought You Had
to Live With*
0-8007-9280-7

Basic biblical guidelines for recog-
nizing if a curse is at work in your
life, then getting out from under
it and living under God's blessing.

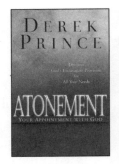

**Atonement, Your
Appointment with God**
0-8007-9277-7

Unpacks what God has provided
for us through the cross, including nine "exchanges"—blessings
in exchange for evils—and five
aspects of deliverance.

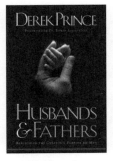

**Husbands
and Fathers**
*Rediscover the Creator's
Purpose for Men*
0-8007-9274-2

Shows in simple terms what it
takes to be a successful husband
and father and bless those closest
to you—your wife and children.

**They Shall Expel
Demons**
*What You Need to Know
about Demons—Your
Invisible Enemies*
0-8007-9260-2

This practical guide to deliverance
from demons discusses seven com-
monly asked questions and how to
receive and minister deliverance.

God Is a Matchmaker
0-8007-9058-8

Examines God's pattern for marriage and shows how it relates to
our lives today. Written with
Derek's wife, Ruth.